I0477485

The Executive Arena

Mastering the Art of *Corporate Politics*, Perceptional Messaging, and Other *Secrets to Success* in Today's Corporate World.

Richard Spector

Table of Contents

It is not the critic who counts; not the man who points out how the strong man stumbles, or where the doer of deeds could have done them better. The credit belongs to the man who is actually in the arena, whose face is marred by dust and sweat and blood; who strives valiantly; who errs, who comes short again and again, because there is no effort without error and shortcoming; but who does actually strive to do the deeds; who knows great enthusiasms, the great devotions; who spends himself in a worthy cause; who at the best knows in the end the triumph of high achievement, and who at the worst, if he fails, at least fails while daring greatly, so that his place shall never be with those cold and timid souls who neither know victory nor defeat.

-Theodore Roosevelt

Acknowledgements

To my amazing wife Sharon. Throughout the years we have been together, you have always supported and believed in me. Even before reading a single word of my book during the initial process, you knew and believed with all your heart it would be a success. Your unwavering love and commitment to our journey together have been the fuel that launched this project, and ultimately brought it to completion. Thank you so much for all you do. I love you.

To Harvey and Jeanette Brown. Thank you for your continued love and support. You both have been an inspiration in more ways than you know. To Stacey and Alan Spector. Thank you for your support and being an important part of our lives. Love to all.

Thank you to Dr. Phillip M. Randall, Steven King, and Veronica Delgado for all your valuable input throughout the entire writing and editing process. Your invaluable advice, not to mention the endorsements, has literally helped shape the content and overall message of this book. Thank you, thank you, thank you.

To my best friends Bill Johnson, Dan Arroyo and Robert Matcham. Whether I was recording music, writing a book, or just needing someone to whom I could vent life's problems, you were always there to at the very least, lend an ear and a beer. Thank you for your friendship.

Thank you to Angie at Pro-eBook Covers. Your work has been absolutely amazing!

Lastly, I would like to give my sincere thanks and gratitude to all the unnamable, yet unforgettable throughout my career... I mean the leaders, supervisors, authors, and mentors that have touched my life, from the naval recruits I've trained to the remarkable peers and subordinates I've worked with side-by-side, thank you. You know who you are. For without the experiences we have shared, this book would not have been possible.

Foreword

Today, most aspiring executives are focused on getting ahead. Unfortunately, too often they rely solely on their credentials, because the system suggests that this is, indeed, the way to the top. However, making one's way to the top requires more than just one's credentials alone. Many believe that getting ahead is based more on luck than preparation and credentials, i.e., a little luck is necessary to make the difference.

More often than not, people think that luck is, in fact, the missing ingredient and may well be the much-needed accompaniment to make the difference in one's assent to and experience in the executive arena. That said, luck is arguably, as a quote from Oscar Wilde, '*the residual of design and desire*'. It is clearly, not mere happenstance.

To get ahead in today's dog-eat-dog world, one must muster all that is available within and outside of one's reach to do so. First, the desire to be on top must be ever present. That is, one must want to get ahead more than anything else. Second, one must organize a plan to do so. Clearly, it is having a plan and the execution of said plan that will matter the most. The thrust of this book by Richard Spector is unquestionably about the manufacturing and/or the making of one's "luck" to getting and staying ahead. It is about being aware of where one is going and rallying all of one's energy and attention to do so. This book advances the much needed and often overlooked aspects of making luck and surviving in the executive arena.

Richard Spector's advice, topic after topic, is about reaching and surviving in the executive arena. It introduces those undiscussed, yet ever present, aspects of successful people, such as identifying, finessing, and where possible, avoiding the political ditches that tend to derail aspirants and plague executive arena members.

Kudos are well deserved for this practical, down-to-earth treatment of the too often unspoken and overlooked truths about the internal workings of the road to and time spent in the executive arena.

For those interested in the creation and manufacturing of the all too illusive ingredients of luck, this is a utility requirement for your toolbox. It provides a three-dimensional lens into how to identify and effectively manage the political domain of the executive arena.

Phillip M. Randall, PhD

International Corporate Speaker, Executive Coach,

and Managing Partner, The Thorndyke Group

Atlanta, GA

November 2018

Introduction

First there was Bill. As a father of three and husband to his wonderful wife Gail, Bill has been with the company for almost ten years now and started his tenure as an entry-level service representative. Bill was promoted to operations supervisor six years ago because he knew his job and knew it well. His operations experience and analytical skills were through the roof. Armed with his extensive formal education, company tenure and business acumen, one would think he would surely one day run the company or, at the very least, achieve a very senior executive position. However, Bill has not been able to rise above a frontline supervisor. He doesn't understand why he can't pull himself out of this rut. He's applied numerous times for other positions in the company, even requested a promotion twice to no avail. In the past six years, aside from his standard annual 3% salary increase, Bill has gone nowhere. Frustrated, he finally convinces himself that it *must* be the company, and it's just not a good fit. He believes that after ten years, the company should have noticed his hard work and cared enough to give him the promotion he deserves. But Bill is wrong. It's not the company.

Then there was Jerry, a young, well-motivated, single man with an active social life. Jerry joined the company as a sales rep, and within six months was promoted to sales manager. Twelve short months later, Jerry was advanced to the director level with a salary commensurate with his new responsibilities. However, after having some "issues" with the leadership, Jerry decided to leave the company. Okay, it was a mutual decision. Jerry landed a new director-level position, and within two years at that company was named vice president, reporting directly to the president/CEO. Again, this came with a significant salary increase. Not bad, huh? Well, don't get too excited about his success just yet. Jerry's success was short lived, and in less than six months in his new VP role, Jerry was terminated. This was his story, employer after employer. In fact, Jerry now makes his living as a DJ, playing in Karaoke bars back in the mid-sized Kansas town he grew up in.

Lastly, meet Samantha. Samantha was a middle-aged mother of three and had been married for nineteen years. She was sharp, had some formal education, and was very good at her job. Samantha began her career as an office assistant, before soon moving into the human resources department. In just eighteen months, Samantha was promoted to HR manager where she finally found her niche. One year later Samantha left the company on good terms for a better position and salary, accepting a director of HR position for a global organization. Two years later? Vice president of human resources, and she's never looked back.

Have you ever thought to yourself, "My God, how did *that* guy ever become a vice president?" Or, "He's in a leadership role? He couldn't lead a Chihuahua on a leash!" Or perhaps you've thought, "Lisa is so smart and has the best ideas. Why isn't she the boss?" You've met these types of people time and time again. In every industry, every company and every department, there are those that climb the corporate ladder with incredible speed, only to find out their success was very short lived. There are others who surely should be promoted but seem (to the novice observer) to never get a fair shake. And, finally, there are those that just seem to do everything right. They ascend the corporate ladder like smoke through a chimney with the flute wide open. They have a glow about them as they smile along the way, advertising to everyone how grateful they are to have such a wonderful life and career.

Believe it or not, Bill, Jerry and Samantha are all true-life examples of what transpires in the corporate world today. But, what *really* separates these individuals from each other? Why such different career results? They all have a decent education, be it formal or hands on, they work hard, and they obviously all have the desire to climb the corporate ladder. So why the significant differences in their career results?

Of course, there are many factors that can affect someone's progress. One's personality, management style, work ethic … Simply too many to list here. Additionally, there are plenty of books, courses, even self-assessments to help you analyze and improve in those areas. But what really differentiates the three examples mentioned previously are two major—or I should say *critical*—factors that are a must if you are to play and *win* in *The Executive Arena*.

1. You must be perceived by others as an expert in your field.

2. You must have highly proficient *Corporate Political Intelligence*.

It goes without saying, but first and foremost you must be *good* at your job. Not just average, but *good!* Additionally, regardless of the vocation you have chosen, you must strive to be *perceived as an expert* in your field, thus developing a positive and influential reputation. How do you know you're perceived as an expert? Answer*: People should come to you for advice, trusting in your guidance, and confident in your reputation.* People should seek out your knowledge, whether through direct contact, or indirectly, via a blog or YouTube channel. It's that simple. Be it through education, hands-on experience, or a combination of both, you must be good at what you do. Yes, you will see some short-term successes by using the skills presented to you in this book, but if you're not good at your job to begin with, you may find your place next to the "Jerrys" of the corporate world. You see, that was Jerry's issue. His *Corporate Political Intelligence* was very high on the charts. He was a master. He knew how to build alliances, chose all his associations wisely, understood how to sell himself and who to do the selling to, and he even mastered the art of *Perceptional Messaging*. (*Perceptional Messaging* is: *The subtle art of influencing how one is perceived by others through intentional and strategic actions.*) We will cover all of this in later chapters. However, it is critical that you understand before we go any further … Jerry just wasn't very good at his chosen vocation. People did not perceive him as an expert (or soon found out he actually wasn't) and thus his apparent successes were short lived.

> **Executive Arena Rule:** You must have the chips just to anti in the game!

Bill, on the other hand, was just the opposite. He was considered an expert in his chosen vocation and was extremely good at his job. In addition, he was an avid reader of business books on leadership and management and kept up to date on business trends and emerging technologies. Contrary to Bill's belief, the company actually loved him. The proof was his being on the job for almost ten years. The company *did* love Bill, but they loved him *in his current position*. They didn't see the value in removing him from his current role and placing him in another, let alone having to find a replacement just as good. When opportunities in the company became available, Bill wasn't even considered as a viable option. Bill lacked *Corporate Political Intelligence*, discussed later.

Lastly, Samantha is pretty much self-explanatory. She was perceived as an expert in her field and had expert *Corporate Political Intelligence*. Her confidant was a senior VP from her previous company. They stayed in touch even after she left and would regularly discuss business issues, solutions and gave advice to each other throughout their careers. She knew how to maneuver around career obstacles and was always setting herself up for success. She was always aware of the *perceptional messages* she was transmitting and understood *The Executive Arena* and how to play the game to *win*!

> **Executive Arena Rule:** Being good at your job is only *half* the battle!

If you are a business professional, aspiring executive or fresh out of college looking to enter the corporate world, this is the book for you. If you're a mid-level manager in your career and looking to climb the corporate ladder, perhaps become a vice president, president or even the CEO of an organization, then keep on reading. This strategic guide will provide you with a completely new lens to look through, allowing you to see what only a few even know exists. If you have ever wondered how to ensure your hard work gets noticed by those who have influence over your career, you've come to the right place. You will be armed with the skills and aptitudes needed to give you the advantage over other players in the game and set yourself up for success.

As if it's some sort of coveted secret, there will be those few unhappy with the information I will be sharing with you. Perhaps they want this valuable information kept concealed, or behind closed doors, afraid that they may be exposed in their shortcomings. Perhaps some may feel they will no longer have the advantage because the information in this book is leveling the playing field. Some may even try to deny they play political games or use the tactics discussed in this book, but I assure you, whether consciously or unconsciously, they do! This is how the corporate world works. When it comes down to you and another person getting a promotion, don't ever underestimate what that other person might do to win. Yes, it's important to "work as a team" and have a strong, *tight-knit* department, but don't ever believe for a second the "team" will matter when it comes to individual success. "I didn't take that promotion and pay raise because I knew you deserved it more than I did" said *no one ever*!

Whatever your reason for picking up this book, rest assured you will be astounded and enlightened at what lies inside this shrouded, yet very real dimension I call *The Executive Arena*.

As we embark on this journey together, it's my sincere hope and my goal to drastically shorten your learning curve by sharing with you many of the skills and experiences that have taken me and other successful executives years to learn. All I ask is that you open your mind to a completely new way of viewing the workplace and how you personally interact within it. Welcome to the improved You. Welcome to the world of highly accomplished business executives and entrepreneurs. Welcome to the select few, the top 5%. Welcome to *The Executive Arena*.

Chapter One: What is *The Executive Arena?*

It was my thirteenth birthday, and my parents were patiently waiting for my decision on where I wanted to go to celebrate. Even at that age, I could tell they were nudging me to decide on what *they* really wanted. They were attempting to secretly manipulate my decision, but I played along. You see, I never had a traditional birthday party growing up. Each year my parents would give me three choices: a fancy restaurant for dinner, an average dinner and a movie, or a play or musical. At a very young age I realized my "birthday" was really an excuse for them to spend some money on themselves and take care of the whole birthday thing in one shot. I don't fault them for it. Actually, I'm grateful that by the time I was in high school, I had seen more plays and musicals than most adults would see in a lifetime and eaten at some pretty fancy Chicago restaurants. "Fancy" being defined as a place a low-income family could afford about once or twice a year. I also, at a very young age (thanks to my parents), learned the art of manipulation and was pretty darn good at it by the age of thirteen. Now, I understand that some of you may be thinking manipulation is a bad word, so call it coaching, guidance, persuasion—whatever makes you feel better. But I'm here to tell you that being able to steer a discussion or group decision to your benefit, and/or in a particular direction, is an invaluable skill when used in the right situation.

That particular day I chose Little Joe's. It was a little restaurant on the south-west side of Chicago that was well known for their lobster. But the lobster wasn't my favorite part of the dinner. It was the huge 250-gallon aquarium situated in the middle of the dining area.

When you walk into a room and see a big, beautiful aquarium, most are impressed by its beauty, and you can't help but stop and stare for a while. The smooth rocks, the ambient lighting, the slow-waving plants, the sometimes-live coral and the brilliantly colored fish all blended into an awe-inspiring spectacle. However, very few people realize the most important element in that tank. The most delicate and vital substance that is the cause of such beauty. It's the water. Yes, the water! It's the unseen. It's the pH level, the hardness, the nitrates and nitrites, the temperature, even the beneficial bacteria all dancing together in perfect harmony to create that life-sustaining ecosystem, which literally brings the aquarium to, and sustains, life. *The Executive Arena* is much like the water in an aquarium. It's extremely important, but, to the untrained, it's a small element not worth the attention, if it's even noticed at all. Most don't give it a second thought. They focus on the fish and the coral, or the rocks and other ornaments, never thinking twice about the very substance that surrounds and connects everything else. If you choose to ignore the water, watch what happens. The filter clogs, and algae forms on the ornaments and glass. The water loses its clarity, and ammonia, nitrates and nitrates spike to dangerous levels. Even the healthiest fish and hardiest coral begin to die.

> **Executive Arena Rule:** Anyone can set up an aquarium, but it takes special skills and experience to keep it going and growing!

So, what actually is *The Executive Arena*? Well, the first step in explaining this critical and vital area you must master to be successful is to first explain what it is *not*. It has nothing to do with what you learned at Harvard Business School or while getting your MBA. It's not related to the college courses you've taken online, the long nights in your dorm cramming for your exam until 2:00 a.m., the skills you've mastered analyzing a detailed P&L (Profit and Loss) statement, or the three-day leadership seminar you attended where you came out thinking *I'm going to frigging kick ass now!* These are all great accomplishments and valuable skills important to your career, but, as mentioned earlier, they are all related to simply being good at your chosen vocation. So, in summary, it's *not* anything to do with your vocational skills or talents.

The Executive Arena is everything else! It's the unseen, the sometimes-unspoken tactics that occur in every organization. It's the conversations that occur behind closed doors. It's the relationships that are built over lunch, on a business trip, or during a game of golf, something I call "shipbuilding." It's the perceptions others have of you, which you must project in a positive way to those who matter to your continued success. It's the relationships you have (or don't have) with your subordinates, your coworkers and, yes, even your superiors. It's about how to get that next promotion ahead of the coworker who is just as qualified as you. It's about how to be assigned the next big project that will surely put you in the limelight. It's about how to come out on top when a coworker (or even a superior) is jealous or feels threatened by your recent performance or success. It's whether or not to attend the next company function or the next party at a colleague's home.

In a nut shell, all these business-related elements, situations, conversations and events, not readily visible or recognizable to the untrained eye, are collectively called *The Executive Arena.* Yes, I'll say it again. These combined elements, situations, conversations and events that surround you throughout your day are *The Executive Arena,* and it is as real as the air you breathe. *The Executive Arena* is the stage on which all corporate political moves are played out, and whether you want to be a good actor in the play or not, you *are* a cast member. Like it or not, your actions, perceptions, conversations, personal and business goals and values are all being observed and analyzed by those around you. I'm sure you have heard from time to time a friend or colleague say, "I don't play those political games" or, "I don't get involved with company drama." Their statement may have been genuine. However, I'm just as sure that the people who said that were either not very successful themselves, or they didn't even realize they *were* playing the game, just not very well.

Unfortunately, that two-word term (corporate politics) has very negative connotations. It's always been a bad word! As we grow older, we're taught to believe that corporate politics is ugly, unethical, sinister, backstabbing and all the nasty little labels you can possibly give it, but that's not necessarily the case. Of course, when someone thinks "politician" they hear the word politics and think "*bad, bad,* run away!" And who can blame them when you take into account our Washington leadership over the past twenty years or so. We've been taught this from a very young age. Remember the terms *brown-noser* or *teacher's pet* or the *boss's favorite?* These were all terms made up by immature adults and kids who, at the time, were oblivious to *The Executive Arena.* They didn't realize the critical importance of understanding and utilizing relationships or shipbuilding. The fact these degrading phrases were even created is proof most realized something was going on. They just didn't understand what it was. Most employees today ask themselves things like: Why is Jill getting all the best projects? How come Mike gets to play golf with the CEO? Because of this, the term *corporate politics* takes center stage. Unfortunately, most still don't truly understand what corporate politics is or how vital it is to embrace it and *The Executive Arena.* They understand corporate politics to mean those little cliques around the office. You know, the same group of employees that eat lunch together while they gossip about who's screwing who; or they spread the rumor that some manager is getting fired tomorrow. It's the same three or four people that hang out together after work, sucking down drinks, bitching about how much the company sucks and "soon, very soon" they are all going to leave but never do. That is *not* corporate politics. That's unwanted and unneeded company drama.

This next statement is of extreme importance, so listen up. If you take one thing from this chapter, then the following statement should be it!

> **Executive Arena Rule:** There is a big difference between *corporate politics* and *company drama*! Never confuse the two!

While at times these two elements may overlap, depending on the situation, they must never be confused. Unfortunately, there are a lot of executives in the business world, some even high on the corporate ladder, that believe corporate politics and company drama (sometimes referred to as office politics) are the same. They are, as a matter of fact, the same people that use the terms leadership and management interchangeably. In both instances, they are wrong. Corporate politics and company drama are opposites! Don't ever forget that. This is where the confusion comes in and, because of this, the actual study of corporate politics and how to successfully master these necessary skills in a positive way has barely been talked or written about in detail, until now. This is where this book comes in.

I'm not saying that corporate politics never gets ugly. It does, and there are and have been plenty of situations where, because of corporate politics, people have been hurt, unjustly and sometimes on purpose. We will discuss the "stomper" (the employee who makes him- or herself look good by making others look bad) and other examples later. For now it's critical you understand the difference between company drama and corporate politics and why things sometimes get ugly.

I hate to use this example because it is a very controversial and political issue, but I figure, what the hell? Let's take guns, for example. Place a gun in the hands of an ethical, caring, professional, well-trained, well-intentioned individual and good things will come from it: the policeman, the soldier, the security guard. Place that same gun in the hands of a lying, cheating, unethical, uncaring asshole and all kinds of problems may arise. The same goes for corporate politics. If you are not very good at your job (or don't care to be), or you honestly can't stand to be around people; or perhaps you're just looking for a way to screw over your boss or colleague— God help us if you're all three!—then put this book down right now! This book is not for you. If you are not an honest, professional and ethical individual with positive values then you are not my audience. You should not be armed with the information presented in this book. If you choose to use this information for less than honorable reasons, your career will be short, with sporadic bursts of success, frosted with continued long-term failure. It's best to just walk away.

My point is: corporate politics can get ugly, but that only happens when you have the wrong person using it. To use a famous *Star Wars* phrase, that's an example of "the Dark Side" of corporate politics. You can become a *Corporate Political Intelligence* master and use *The Executive Arena*'s power in a positive way to advance your career and your organization at the same time.

Since you haven't closed this book, that tells me you are a true professional, or at least aspiring to be. You know you are good at your job, and you care enough about yourself and those around you to be the best you can be. Just taking this book off the shelf means you are seeking additional learning. You are looking for new ways to improve, to grow, and to expand your knowledge to the point of someday becoming the teacher or mentor to others while you achieve your dreams of success. Something a mentor told me a long time ago, and it's worth sharing with you right now is this:

> **Executive Arena Rule:** The greats never stop learning. If you ever reach a point in your career when you think to yourself, "I know all I need to know," then your career is over. You should strive to be a Lifelong Learner, for you can learn something new every day.

We will go into more detail in a later chapter, but it's important you understand that corporate politics is alive and well, and it's a vital area you must learn to navigate. It exists in all types of business. Small, medium, large, local, international, private, public, manufacturing, education, retail, technology, healthcare, research, even mom and pop's small shop around the corner. Wherever you work, if you are to achieve that top position, you must learn, implement, and master *Corporate Political Intelligence*. It's one of the critical tools in your *Executive Arena* tool box. Some people are good at it. Some are playing the game (badly) and they don't even realize it until they are no longer employed. Some have used corporate politics unknowingly, have seen some success and now just need to hone their skills. A few others, a very small percentage, are *Executive Arena* masters, and they have continued and sustained success throughout their careers. You can become politically savvy, and that's exactly what I intend to teach you in this book.

In an article from <u>money.com</u> titled "How Office Politics Works" Jane McGrath writes:

Office politics is at the core of all organizations. Paying attention to it can be just as important as fulfilling the responsibilities written in your job description. If you aren't on the watch for it or don't tactfully engage in it, you could jeopardize your career and watch your hard work and loyalty go down the drain.

She goes on to say,

It's so important that the category of <u>organizational politics</u> has blossomed into its own field of study within psychology. Here's why: The distribution of power and the appearance of fairness in the workplace impact how satisfied employees are with their jobs. Believing you and your opinions make a difference may make you happier in your career and in your life.

Take note of the words "the *appearance* of fairness" and "*believing* your opinions matter." There's that darn *Perceptional Messaging* at work again.

Strong *Corporate Political Intelligence* is one of *The Executive Arena* tools and main reasons some individuals become extremely successful even with little to no formal education. You've heard the term "street-smart" or he went to "the school of hard knocks." These idiomatic phrases refer to the non-formal education one received (usually painfully) through life's ups and downs, coming up through the ranks the hard way and having to learn by doing. Don't misunderstand me. I'm not belittling a good formal education. It's surely *one* viable way of becoming an expert in your chosen vocation. As mentioned before, you must be good at your chosen vocation, so do whatever it takes to make sure that happens. However, *being good at your job is only half the battle*! Some people became *Corporate Political Intelligence* masters because it was all they had. It was their edge. Having no degree they entered the race a few laps behind their formally educated counterparts. It's only logical these *Corporate Political Intelligence* masters learned how to play the game quickly and play it well. Having strong *Corporate Political Intelligence* means you know how to set yourself up for success. You've learned how to position yourself for the best opportunities and ensure other's perceptions of you are always positive.

There are plenty of people with incredible *Corporate Political Intelligence* and no college degree. But it's important to remember, as discussed earlier, that the public also perceived the following people as experts in their field. Here are just a few examples:

- Bob Proctor, millionaire, motivational speaker, bestselling author, and co-founder of Life Success Publishing, attended two months of high school.

- Charles Culpeper, owner and CEO of Coca Cola, dropped out of high school.

- Henry Ford, founder, Ford Motor Company, never attended college.

Bill Gates, Walt Disney, Wolfgang Puck, Simon Cowell, Rachel Ray, Robert Downey Jr., Richard Branson ... the list goes on and on! I could fill this book with similar examples. These people never obtained a college degree. Most never even stepped foot on a campus, but they all have something in common. They were all perceived as experts in their field, and they all understood *The Executive Arena*!

Now visualize, just for a moment, what your success would look like if you were perceived as an expert in your field, as well as a *Corporate Political Intelligence* master. Imagine the positive and strong relationships you would have with those in your charge as well as your superiors. Imagine being able to recognize the real movers and shakers in your organization, and utilize that knowledge to your benefit with integrity. Imagine having control over your next raise or promotion, instead of wishing or hoping it will come "someday." This is my goal for you as we journey through the chapters of this book together. It may not be the easiest book you've ever read, but I assure you the concepts presented are simple in nature and easy to implement. I will be here with you as we explore and learn to master the skills and tactics presented in the following pages. All I ask is that you open your mind to a new way of viewing the workplace. Accept the fact that whatever your upbringing, education or current situation, understanding and implementing the tools provided in this book can and will have a significant impact on your career and life goals. It can be life transforming.

Over the past twenty-five years I have observed, dabbled, absorbed, implemented and become a lifelong student of what I now call *The Executive Arena*. It's not an exact science; it's an art, a skill, and, like other critical management skills, it can be learned! I have seen it in action and seen its success countless times, many of which will be presented in this book. In short, it works! My last position in the corporate world, before I retired and became an author, was as vice president of a very successful business college, with a salary well into six figures. Along the way, I've held higher and more challenging senior management positions, including running my own consulting company. But to go from being a high school dropout to holding successful senior management positions in the education industry (among others) is unheard of. Yes, spending ten years in the US Navy got me off the streets of Chicago and gave me the basic leadership skills I needed in the beginning, but, all in all, not too shabby for a kid from the south side of Chicago who had no chance of going to college. My parents were poor and had little to no interest in my schooling. They never attended any open houses, school plays, science fairs, or even realized I had won first place in a state-wide architectural drafting competition, or singing competition, or whatever. They were focused on themselves, and all the problems that go along with just scraping by, living from paycheck to paycheck. But I knew deep inside there was more to life than just getting by. I didn't have the money to go to college, so I had to do the best I could with what I had. And I did. More importantly, so can you!

I don't mention these personal things to brag or for sympathy. I bring them up to hammer home the fact that regardless of your education, situation or where you are at in your career today, you can begin to change your position and direction in a positive way right now. To go from a McDonald's employee in Chicago, to a senior vice president living in La Jolla California, to retired and an author at fifty-three is not luck. It's never too late. Believe me, if I can achieve the things I have, so can you! Let's turn the pages together and put *you* in control of your destiny.

Points to remember:

1. Do not confuse corporate politics with company drama. They are *not* the same thing.
2. Corporate politics is the unseen, sometimes unspoken, actions and tactics that occur in every organization. *The Executive Arena* is the stage on which all corporate plays are acted out.
3. Becoming a *Corporate Political Intelligence* master is critical to your success! Like it or not, you are a cast member. You must learn to play the game, and play it well, or you will lose. It's that simple.
4. You can engage in corporate politics in a positive way. *Corporate Political Intelligence* is a management skill you *can* learn.
5. To achieve long-term success in *The Executive Arena*, you must first be good at your chosen vocation, or at the very least be constantly working at it. If you are not, then the successes you will experience from this book will be short lived.
6. Like those who've gone before you, from Henry Ford to Rachel Ray, you too can be a huge success even without a degree! A formal education (while the most popular route) is only one path to becoming a subject matter expert. However, there is no road to bypass *Corporate Political Intelligence*. You must become a *Corporate Political Intelligence* master if you are to rise successfully into the senior management ranks and beyond.

Chapter Two: Knowing the Players and How They Move.

Before you can successfully enter *The Executive Arena*, and become a competitive player, you must first learn about the different players or *pieces* used in the game and how they move. Let's take the game of checkers for starters. The object of the game is to move your little round disk-like pieces, in only a diagonal direction, locked on the same color squares throughout the game, in an attempt to "jump" your opponent's pieces, until someone runs out of moves. The winner is determined by who has the most pieces left on the board, or who lost the most pieces in the process. Kind of a glass-half-full or half-empty way of thinking. But, in the end, someone loses and someone wins. While there is some strategic approach to the game, it's very simplistic in nature. That's why it's such a popular game among children, and one of the first games most of us learned to play at a young age, aside from tic-tac-toe. Comparing checkers to *The Executive Arena* is like comparing a bicycle to a Mercedes Benz. They both will get you from point A to point B, but the skills and experience needed to successfully operate and maintain the Mercedes are far greater than those needed for the bike. Not to mention the slight difference in performance. This is how most people in the workforce today view the corporate environment. A bunch of pieces on the board, each doing their own thing. You move here and there, make a jump here and there, and, hopefully, in the end, you've made enough good moves or decisions to be successful. Most view the corporate environment as very simplistic, like the game of checkers. Go to work, get your check, come home, hope for the best.

Hold that thought, and now let's examine the ultimate strategic game of chess. A chessboard has the same number of squares, the same size, shape and layout as the checker board. It's the same workplace, the same department, company or organization. However, what has drastically changed is the pieces, the players, the employees and, ultimately, the two executives sitting on each side of the boardroom table. Everyone within your organization has a different way of operating, depending on the situation they are faced with. Much like the different pieces of a chess game, each piece has its own unique characteristics and way of operating within the game. There are no restrictions to the playing board colors. It's the makeup of the piece, or the person, that will determine how it can be moved. All pieces, from the pawn to the queen, play a valuable role in winning the game. What's important here is that *you* are able to recognize and learn the role each piece (or employee) plays in the game. What type of employee are they? What drives them and how do they operate? What's their motivational engine? Do they strive to help others succeed? Are they only looking out for themselves? Do they steal others' ideas and claim them as their own? Are they mentors or dictators?

Social Astuteness Exercise: The following exercise is to get you thinking about those around you and their actions. It's designed to increase your social astuteness. Social astuteness is the ability to read and anticipate situations. It allows you to prepare, adapt and tailor your behavior based on the people and conditions around you. It's about being good at sensing the motivations and possible hidden agendas of others. It's about instinctively receiving non-verbal messages through body language, facial expressions and other not so obvious mediums.

From *The Executive Arena* standpoint, all employees fall within one or more of the following six categories, which, coincidentally, is the same number as the different types of pieces in chess. As we learn about these different players in the game, think about the people you have met in the past or currently know that fit into one of these categories. Be honest and ask yourself which character traits listed below do you possess and to what degree? Lastly, remember that people can fall into more than one category, if even temporarily based on the situation. Let's review each player.

1. **The Mentor:** *Great leaders don't try to be heroes, they strive to create them!*

The driving force of a mentor is to help those around them be successful. This type of leader believes that if those in his/her charge are successful, then they in turn will be successful. They view themselves as the boat on the water. As the tide rises, they are lifted up along with it. The majority of their day is spent coaching, training and supporting their subordinates, to ensure those in their charge have all the tools necessary to be successful. It's a trait that every great leader possesses to some degree, and rightly so, as it ranks fairly high in the "Great Leader Traits" category. However, being too much of a mentor can also hinder their ability to lead effectively. A mentor is a people person, which is good. However, at times they can be empathetic to a fault. Because of this, some mentors are very slow to reprimand or write someone up for poor performance, let alone terminate someone when it's needed. They go out of their way to give that employee a second chance or even a third and fourth, when all evidence points to the fact they should be terminated. They see themselves as a rescuer or fixer, and their belief in how they operate is strengthened even if in only a single instance they prove successful. In other words, they gave someone a second chance and it worked. Unfortunately, in many situations the mentor is so focused on "fixing" an individual, they fail to see how keeping that employee on board has affected others, as well as the company as a whole. In summary, they can be easily blinded by their own drive to help others. Don't get me wrong. Being a mentor is a very valuable and honorable trait to have, but you must have balance between mentorship and the greater good of your team, department or company.

Learn to recognize who the mentors are in your company, or who they were in past experiences. True mentors are often found in the higher ranks of middle to upper management, and even among some presidents and CEOs. Take a few minutes now and make a mental note (or write down on paper) those whom you believe are mentors, or at least have shown those type of traits more often than not. They can be those you've known or worked with in the past, or perhaps they are in your current employ. Think back to instances when you have seen them in action. What were they like? Did they pride themselves on being a coach to others? Have you seen the mentor trait cloud their judgment or yours? Do this now before moving on to the next player in the game.

2. **The Stomper**: *Excuse me while I step on your shoulders ... Don't worry, it won't hurt!*

The stomper, according to the simplest definition, likes to step on others. They don't do this just because they're mean. They are the person who goes out of their way to make others look bad, *in an attempt to make themselves look good.* In other words, the worse you look, the better they look. Instead of rising above the crowd on their own merits, they have a strong desire to degrade others on their team, or anyone whom they regard as a threat to their own success, hoping to stand out as the victor. Most times, but not always, you will see this characteristic displayed in those who are not very good at their job. They have some confidence issues regarding their ability, so they compensate in the only way they know how. Most stompers are the start of, or play a significant role in, the rumor mill. They are the gossipers around the office, spending more time and energy fueling fires than focusing on becoming a better employee or manager. However, this is not always the case. While you may think the stomper is easily recognized, some are brilliant in their quest. The target of such a person may not even know they are being stomped on.

Remember Jerry from the Introduction? Jerry was a vice president for a tech company and was my boss (twice actually) early in my management career. I had worked for him in retail before he recruited me over to a high-tech training company back in 2000. We worked extremely well together and had a great relationship even outside of working hours. That is, up until the point when he realized I was being considered for a VP role as well. Oh no! I would be his equal? Up until this point in our working relationship, Jerry was always one level above me, and he was content as long as I remained his subordinate. We spent a lot of time talking to each other about our career goals. He was a confidant of sorts. We will discuss the confidant in a later chapter.

I knew he was a stomper, so one day, in a sort of joking attitude, I told him, "Tell you what, Jerry. I'll continue to work hard to ensure you get promoted. Just make sure you take me up the ladder with you."

"You have a deal," he responded with a big shit-eating grin. We both wanted to move up and someday run the company. In fact, we would joke over drinks or dinner about who would be CEO and who would be president someday. I assumed we were just joking around. I was wrong. Jerry took my ambition as a serious threat, and, once I was finally promoted to his level, vice president, his attitude and our relationship changed drastically. I didn't know it at the time, but much later I found out Jerry did all he could to slip in little negatives and falsehoods to the president and other senior team members about me, designed to belittle my skills and achievements. This happened numerous times over golf, dinner, after a meeting; whenever he saw an opportunity to get another jab in. Of course, all his work was for nothing, and he was never promoted to president. But he was successful in ensuring I didn't get that position either. You know how Jerry's story ends, but I tell you this so you completely understand: not all stompers are easily recognizable. Sometimes it's the person you would least expect.

So, once again, have you run across a stomper? Take some time and write down those people you believe may fit into this category.

3. **The Steady Eddie**: *I'm a good worker, I'm never late, just give me my check.*

Like the pawn in a chess game, the Steady Eddie normally constitutes the greatest number in any organization. The Steady Eddie is neither an overachiever nor an underperformer. They are, as the term indicates, steady in their performance and lifestyle. Additionally, as you might have guessed, a majority of Steady Eddies have no interest in moving up the corporate ladder. They are not striving to move into management, nor are they trying to make a big name for themselves or be the center of attention. They simply come to work, do their job, collect their paycheck and go home. And that's okay! If the majority of your staff shows up on time and does their job, you're in good hands. They are content with their current situation, and most try not to get involved with strategic thinking, company direction, thinking "outside the box," etc. Nevertheless, the Steady Eddie is not a bad characteristic. Quite the opposite. Consider a standard, mid-sized sales team of, say, twenty people. Within this team, you have your top 5–10%. They are your superstars, your overachievers. They always exceeding their ever-increasing sales goals, month after month, year after year. Their energy and desire to be the best is built into their DNA. Of course, with high performance comes high maintenance, but the tradeoff is well worth it to any good sales manager. If you have three or four of these top performers, you're doing well. Then you have your bottom 20%. This group is a combination of both *newbies*, who are still in training and learning the ropes, and the underperformer, the one who just might not work out. Because high turnover is a norm in any sales force, this bottom 20–30% is constantly rotating in, up or out of the team. That leaves the middle group. The final 60% or so are the Steady Eddies. They do the minimum required—they hit their goal or darn close to it—and they do this month after month, year after year.

They are not the superstar and their numbers are nothing to write home about, but you can count on their specific number every month. Because they make up the majority of your team (strength in numbers), your overall team is solid. Get the picture? At first glance, the Steady Eddie doesn't seem all that important to the organization, but, just like the pawn in chess, while simple in design, and the majority, they are a necessary player. Some managers will look at a Steady Eddie as *lacking ambition*, or not a "team player," but that's just bad management and another book (coming soon) entirely. If you have ten Steady Eddies on your team, and you know each will produce at least $50k in sales each month, then you know next month you will have a minimum of $500k, and you haven't even started. It makes budgeting much easier and allows you to focus on the bottom 20–30%, which is where your focus should always be.

CRITICAL NOTE: The worst thing you can do is try to turn a genuine Steady Eddie into a high performer. It won't work, and even good-intentioned management attempts could push a consistent performer into the bottom 20%, soon to be gone from the company altogether.

Another trait of the Steady Eddie, more relevant to *The Executive Arena*, is that *they go with the flow*. Like a chameleon, they will jump on board the train that has the most votes, or the most support. When a decision needs to be made, and there are two sides to the argument, more often than not the Steady Eddie will side with the majority. It's not a negative trait. It's just that they are looking to blend in, not cause any waves, do their job and collect their check. Knowing that this is how Steady Eddies operate can prove beneficial when trying to rally the troops for an important project or company initiative.

Lastly, the Steady Eddie exists in every department, division, company, and in every industry. From human resources to marketing, from retail to hospitality, they exist for a reason. So be grateful they are there, and for God's sake don't try to change them into an ambitious top performer. It will never work. Just recognize them for who they are and understand their role in the game. Now take a few moments and add to your list those at your company (or from your past) who you believe are Steady Eddies. It should be your biggest list of names thus far.

4. **The Dictator:** *I'm in charge of my department, and it needs to stay that way!*

At first read, you may think the dictator is someone who likes to bark orders. While that is one small apparent trait, it's not the main reason for the player's label. Firstly, on a positive note, the dictator will always follow the rules. They are sticklers concerning company policy, and you can rest assured they will not allow any deviation once company processes and procedures are put into place. In short, they are creatures of habit. But that initial positive perception is just on the surface. More often than not, the dictator has a prodigious fear of losing their job. They are constantly trying to prove their value to others, mainly to his/her superiors, when in most cases they don't need to. Most dictators are easily recognized once they move into management, for a couple reasons. First, dictators are not very open to change. Once they've become very secure in their position and confident of the processes in place and the people on their team, any changes, even slight, to the "way things have always been" puts the dictator on edge. Worse, any significant changes, such as company growth, or a chain-of-command restructure, will put the dictator on the offensive.

Second, because of the constant urge to prove their value, the dictator believes that, as the department head, or "the boss," they must always be the *smartest one on the team*. They come from a school of thought that teaches that because they are in charge, they should know more than their subordinates. That can be detrimental to any organization. The dictator is afraid to hire anyone who, in their eyes, could do their job better than they can. They will unconsciously, or sometimes consciously, turn away any candidate whom they perceive to have greater skills or experience than themselves. In short, the dictator refuses to surround themselves with great talent, which is a huge problem. Let's put it another way. Any great leader will know their own strengths and weaknesses. They know in great detail what challenges they face and they hire those who can supplement or *fill in* where they may fall short. It's how you build a solid and successful team. No one is perfect, and no one person becomes successful on their own.

I remember back in Kansas City. We were two weeks away from the grand opening of our new location. I had recently moved my family from Chicago for the opportunity to be part of this high-tech start-up company so it was important this venture was a success. We had hired all the staff, and they were well trained and ready to go. The success of this grand opening would set the bar going forward for sales and ultimately profits. Honestly, I wasn't sure what to do. I had already scheduled some TV and print advertising, purchased some billboards, and done some local grass-roots canvasing, announcing our grand opening. But we needed more. Nothing I had done so far would guarantee people would show up. What did we do? We called a lunch meeting with the entire staff. We brought in pizza and told the staff we needed ideas for a kick-ass grand opening, and we were not leaving until we had a solid plan in place. If it took an hour to come up with a plan, great! If it took us until 10:00 p.m. that night, then that's what it would take. To make a long story short, the grand opening was a huge success! The mayor of Kansas City came out to do a ribbon-cutting ceremony (mostly because he knew a radio station would be there), while we had the top radio station on site doing a live radio remote, advertising the free dogs and burgers we were giving away, as well as the mayor's presence! The synergy was perfect! We brought in tons of new business, the radio station got to interview the mayor and be involved in the community, and the mayor got some free publicity! It was a win-win-win!

My point is, I didn't come up with any of those ideas. They came from my team. If I thought I was the smartest person on my team, I would have never called that meeting. We would not have broken the company record for a start-up and would never have been able to set the company standards for future locations. "You didn't do a great job, your staff did" said no one ever! Imagine if a president or CEO refused to hire an HR manager because he/she knew more about employment law then he did? Or a CFO who turned away a controller because they knew double-book accounting, something the CFO struggled with in college? In closing, the dictator's urge to remain in power, unwillingness to change and unwillingness to learn can be costly to the organization, and makes the dictator one of the most destructive players in the game. Do you know any dictators? You know what to do. Fire them all! Just kidding. Add them to your list. We will reference this list in later pages.

5. **The Trigger Finger:** *I don't have the time to coach you, you're fired!*

Let me start by painting a picture for you. I took a job back in 1995 working for a small start-up company in Chicago as the director of sales. My first directive was to expand and build their small (at the time) sales force. The New Hire Training Process was to consist of one day of orientation, one week of shadowing a senior sales executive, combined with two weeks of formal sales training. Basically a three-week training program before they were on their own. Once that was completed successfully, the new sales rep was to be given his own office, a dedicated phone line, a computer and two days of training on their new sales management software.

It was a good plan, and the above description was something we told all possible candidates over the next two weeks. Are you with me so far? Good. Now fast forward two weeks. I had brought on three really sharp candidates, and all had completed the orientation and were currently shadowing the senior sales executives. The owner of the company, to whom I reported directly, came into my office and said, "Let's get the new people some leads and get them on the phone." I looked up at him, I'm guessing with a confused look, because his response was, "Did I stutter or something? We need sales and we need them now. We don't have time for this drawn-out training process." I clearly and abruptly told him, "They are not ready." But after several minutes of trying to convince him it was a mistake, I reluctantly followed his direction, and figured I would prove my point later, armed with the results from a lead-conversion report. Or so I thought.

After one week of hovering over my newbies on the phone, trying to guide them in real time the best I could, and making a couple sales myself along the way, each one actually made a sale that week! Now the standard benchmark was 3–4 in a single week per rep, but I was pleasantly surprised. With no training whatsoever, they were each able to pull off a solid sale. They had no personal phone, no office, and no computer. Armed only with a yellow legal pad, a shared phone and a pen, they pulled it off! I took this report to the owner, and strongly suggested we now get them back on the training plan. I explained, "They pulled this off with no training. Now imagine what they could do with the proper training!" Well, his response blew me away. "We don't have time to babysit these new people! They aren't working out. Fire them, and let's get some new blood in here!" What the fuck? I believe I actually said those words out loud, something I'm not very proud of even to this day, but it just kind of came out. How could it not?

So, I won't bore you with the details. Let's just say the conversation that followed (if you can call it a conversation) was not pleasant. All three reps were terminated as he requested, followed shortly by my resignation. This company, by the way, is no longer in business, closing their doors about eighteen months later.

The trigger finger is the exact opposite of the mentor. They don't understand the difference between leadership and management. The trigger finger believes it's a lot easier to just fire someone and start over, rather than coaching and training someone. Like a cattle call (and I've witnessed that type of hiring as well), they will hire a bunch of people, throw them against the wall, and, with little to no training or tools, will watch to see who sticks. It's a process that does work initially, but at great cost to the company because of extremely high turnover; not to mention the human aspect and unethical cultures it creates. Write this next statement down. Burn it into your memory because it's extremely important, and if you haven't guessed by now, I'm very passionate about it.

> **Executive Arena Rule:** An employee has an *obligation* to provide a good service, so the company can do its best! However, the employer has an even greater *obligation* to provide the environment, training and tools necessary so the employee *can* provide his/her best!

The trigger finger believes the employer/employee contractual agreement is one sided. They live in a world where *the employee should be lucky they even have a job*. A world where they are doing the employee a *favor* by even paying them. While (thank God) the trigger finger isn't widespread, they are out there. They are quick to "pull the trigger" when things aren't going their way. It's a way to shift blame to anyone but themselves when things go wrong.

One of those reps we terminated filed a lawsuit and sued for six months salary, including potential commissions, and *won*! Including legal fees, it cost the company about $48,000, all because we needed those three extra sales, which equated to just over $15,000. That's $15k in sales, not profit. That $48k came directly off their bottom line.

Lastly, it should be noted here that a trigger finger can actually and unknowingly create dictators and thieves (discussed next) beneath them. You will find most trigger fingers in sales management positions as turnover is higher in sales than most other parts of the organization. Being quick to fire can easily put those in their charge on the defensive. Employees who are always having to worry about job security are unproductive. This is unhealthy. Team members can begin to feel the need to further prove their value in any way possible to keep their job, including those who are already doing very well in their position. It can create an environment of stress and distrust, and breed unhealthy competition, leading to increased and unnecessary turnover, not to mention reduced productivity. It's easy for the sales manager to fall into the "I don't have the time to train properly" rut, due to the constant but normal pressure to hit monthly sales goals from the powers that be. I hope this next list is small, but, once again, add to your list or make a mental note of any trigger fingers you may have known.

6. **The Thief:** *Finally, we come to the last player on the board, the thief.*

To varying degrees, the thief is very common in *The Executive Arena*. You may be thinking that the thief is a stealer of another's ideas. Well, you would be somewhat correct. The thief, somewhat like the dictator, is looking for ways to improve his value to the company or an individual. However, as we previously discussed, it may not always be so visible. The thief is not someone who breaks into the company suggestion box to browse through the little folded pieces of paper in an attempt to find a golden idea to pitch to the president (though, yes, I have witnessed that firsthand). The motivation behind such actions is not fear, as it is with the dictator. It's greed or envy. The thief wants to move up, not necessarily just keep his/her job. While present in the ranks of the general employee, the thief becomes an issue when they are in a supervisory or management role.

Let's revisit the Kansas City opening again. Remember, I went to my team for suggestions on how to have a ... I believe the term was kick-ass grand opening? Of course, I told my boss what I did, and I gave full credit to my team. However, a thief could have easily picked up the phone, called the president of the company and said, "I have a great plan for our Kansas City grand opening," never mentioning where the ideas came from. Well, frankly, that's exactly what happened. While I did the right thing, *my* boss at that time picked up the phone and called the president. I didn't know he passed off my team's ideas as his own, of course, until two

41

weeks later when I personally got a call from the president. He was responding to an email I sent out company wide, where I thanked "my employees for coming together as a team, and developing a wonderful grand opening plan, resulting in the company's best grand opening to date." Do you see what happened here? That's *Corporate Political Intelligence* in action: passively ensuring your efforts (or your team's) are noticed.

Now the president didn't say to me, "Hey, Joe said these were his ideas," like some scorned school kid upset that his lunch money was stolen. Not at all. He called me to say great job, but during our *informal* conversation, I remember him asking a few probing questions. "So, look, I loved the live radio remote you guys did. Who came up with that idea?" he asked. "That was Kelly, my new sales rep," I replied proudly. "I was a little afraid of what it might cost, but once I got the numbers and realized it was within our budget, it was a no brainer," I explained.

There are many different players in the game, all maneuvering for the best possible position at any given time. Being more perceptive of what goes on behind closed doors, what may be said during private phone conversations and through emails, can be overwhelming at first. Being more observant of the actions of those around you will, over time, increase your social astuteness. You will begin to realize, if you haven't already, that there is so much more that can affect your success than just job performance. It can, and sometimes does, get very malicious in the competitive world of *The Executive Arena*. Not unlike chess, people are always fighting for their position on the game board, trying to think two or three moves ahead of the next player and controlling "center square." This is why being alert to your surroundings and increasing your social astuteness is critical. It can get hostile in the workplace. What? Hostile work environment? Perhaps some of you HR professionals are saying, "I'm not sure I'd call that a hostile work environment," and to a degree they would be correct. But they would also, to some degree, be wrong. When it comes to corporate politics, the actions some of these individual players take are not always obvious, even after an official investigation from a complaint to HR. You can't track the results or repercussions on a spreadsheet. It's not as blatant as someone making sexual advances or reporting to work under the influence of alcohol. It's not normally an infraction found in the employee manual. However, these types of unethical tactics can and do have devastating effects on people and the organization. Have you ever had an employee resign and that resignation catch you completely off guard? How about a no call/no show from an employee you thought was doing pretty well? Or what about the top performer, whose performance, for no obvious reason, took a turn for the worse? Is turnover high in a particular department and you can't put your finger on the problem?

Of course, there are many reasons for such situations, but my point is that there may be reasons that, up until now, you have not considered. It's not always *black and white*. In fact, in most cases it's not. Just because an employee investigation didn't find any proof of malicious intent, doesn't mean it doesn't exist. Sometimes these political tactics or behaviors are very covert and go undetected by even the most experienced professionals. Just remember the old saying: People don't leave the organization ... People leave people!

As I bring this chapter to a close, there is something I must share with you. In the beginning of this chapter and throughout, I asked you to begin making a list, at least a mental one. After each *player* description, I asked you to write down the names of employees, current or in the past, and tag them with a certain player description. The mentor, the stomper, the Steady Eddie, the dictator, the trigger finger and, lastly, the thief. However, tagging those names with a label was not the most important part of the exercise. *It was the names you wrote down that were of the utmost importance.* Don't look at the labels or traits as a type of person or player. Look at the above six labels as tactics, maneuvers or actions. The mentor, the stomper and all the rest are not nouns, they're *verbs*! You see, while most people will have a dominant trait, anyone can enact any one of those behaviors when faced with a particular situation. The real exercise was the people you listed, not the labels, and to help exercise your social astuteness muscle.

As you stopped reading from time to time, contemplating what you were learning, and thought to yourself, *Bob is a stomper*, or *Sally is a dictator*, or you were possibly a mentor, you were building a list of great importance that we will reference as we progress through this guide. It's exactly what I hoped you would d. Whether they are subordinates, coworkers, or superiors, you listed them for a reason. Take another look at your list. You are in some way directly or indirectly involved with them as you perform your day-to-day functions on the job. Your involvement may be more with some and less with others, but all of them, for one reason or another, were important enough to list and, thus, have some level of impact on your career progression. So, grab a beer, have a martini, or make yourself a banana split and congratulate yourself because *the people you listed are those who could have or will have the biggest impact on your career!* Remember who they are, even if they are past coworkers. Know how they operate and commit them to memory. It is those people, those *players*, who will be vital to your success as we continue to move you closer to becoming a formidable opponent in *The Executive Arena.*

Points to Remember:

1. Social astuteness is the ability to read and anticipate situations. It allows you to prepare, adapt and tailor your behavior based on the people and conditions around you. It's about being good at sensing the motivations and possible hidden agendas of others.

2. Sometimes political tactics or behaviors are very covert and go undetected by even the most experienced professionals. Just remember the old saying: People don't leave the organization… People leave people!

3. The traits listed above are not nouns, they're *verbs!* While most people will have a dominant trait, anyone can enact any one of those behaviors when faced with a particular situation.

Chapter Three: *Perceptional Messaging* - at Work

The classroom was silent. The only white noise I can remember hearing was the air blowing through the old, rusting AC vents in the ceiling, while the sound of her heels echoed off the concrete walls as they connected with the hardwood floor beneath each step. Every student was deeply focused on their work as she walked very slowly up and down the aisles between our desks. With her arms crossed and posture very upright and formal, she would glance down at each of us as she passed, making sure we were studying intensely as she had previously requested. Engulfed in her arms, almost hidden from sight, was the sacred candy jar she carried with her. If she felt you were doing as told, she would place a piece of candy on your desk, as if to say, "Thank you for following orders." Looking back on that fourth-grade experience, it's as if I was one of Pavlov's dogs, involved in one of her own conditioning experiments. But at the time I didn't mind. In fact, I enjoyed the challenge. Not everyone received this honorary piece of candy as she passed. If my memory serves me correctly, about one quarter of the class would benefit on any given day. But I did manage to get that wonderful piece of candy ... every ... single ... time.

Mrs. Toomey, my fourth-grade teacher, had the reputation for being very strict on her students, even *mean* from a fourth-grade student perspective. But I honestly never felt that way. When she gave the order, "Time for self-study," my classmates would scramble to find something of importance to do. Some would grab a book to read (not a bad choice), some would decide to just draw or color (no candy for you), while others would work on completing homework, so they wouldn't have to do it later that evening. But I was a little different. Maybe even a little screwed up, because my goal wasn't just to read, or to complete homework ahead of schedule. My ultimate goal was to get that damn piece of candy! So, in my infinite wisdom (not), I would grab three text books, none having any connection to the others, and place them open on my desk. Armed with a pencil, I would systematically copy a sentence from each book, one at a time, to my writing tablet. By tablet, I mean an 8½" X 11" paper writing pad. Tablets or iPads, as we know them today, didn't exist back then. As Mrs. Toomey passed my desk, she would see the fingers of my left hand underlining a specific sentence in a book, while my right hand copied that sentence to my tablet, as if I were taking notes. Once that sentence was completed, I would move to another sentence in the next book. Down came that piece of candy every time.

Okay, I wasn't really learning a damn thing, right? I was just faking it. Pretending I was studying wasn't doing me any good whatsoever. Or was it? You see, I remember getting my first semester report card from fourth grade. Unlike today, it was hand written on thick paper, almost cardboard by today's standards, and sealed in a small manila envelope. My parents, of course, would have to sign it, and I would return it to school the next day. I always received decent grades, mostly As and Bs, but that's not what's important here. It was Mrs. Toomey's comments on this particular report card that has burned a lesson into my memory even to this day. The comments read: "Richard is extremely clever. He's one of my favorite students … and he knows it!" Wait, what? "And he knows it"? I understand and frankly love the fact that she called me clever. That's a bonus. Who wouldn't? And I'm totally cool with her saying I'm one of her favorites, but to say "And he knows it" sheds a very interesting light on this chapter.

Yeah, I knew she liked me. What I didn't realize was that she knew I was just "acting" as though I was studying. *She understood and accepted the fact that I was putting in just as much effort towards her "perception" of me as I did on my actual school work.* Moreover, she didn't call me out on that fact. She never said, "Okay, Richard, now let's do something constructive. I know the game you're playing." Instead, she continuously rewarded me for my efforts. Why did she do that? What's the overall lesson here?

Well, it's important to first remind you of something once again. Initially, as mentioned numerous times before, you must first be good at your job! You can't suck at what you do, or not care about your job, and expect to make it to the top. A lot of people have tried, and all of them have failed in the long run. The true lesson here is that *perception is more than half the battle!* How others in the workplace *perceive* you is absolutely critical, and just as important, if not more important, than your actual job performance. Remember the term "fake it till you make it"? That rings true here to some degree and will continue to be a key element in *The Executive*

Arena. Actively monitoring your reputation in the corporate world and governing how others perceive you at work is critical to your success, and it's an essential element in becoming a *Corporate Political Intelligence* master.

For example, let's dabble a bit here in the realm of sexual harassment. You are sitting at your desk when Barbara, your coworker, walks through the door in a beautiful summer dress. You are impressed! She looks amazing in that dress, and so you decide to tell her as much. You turn to her and say, "Hey, Barb, you look amazing in that dress," and you give her a thumbs-up. No harm no foul, right? Wrong. Let's say your comment to her was genuine, heartfelt and innocent. You truly meant to give her a compliment. However, Barbara felt very uncomfortable. Because you never reacted that way before, she concluded you were singling her out in front of the other employees and reported the situation to human resources. I'm not going to get into what may or may not happen, or who was wrong and who was right in that situation. Let's leave that to the HR professionals. What I will tell you is this. It doesn't really matter what your true intentions were. What matters in this situation and the corporate world, what matters in *The Executive Arena*, is *her* "perception" of you in that particular situation.

Truth or rumor, fact or fiction, *perception* plays a critical role in your success! If you are to master one chapter in this book, this is it! You must understand that everything you do, everything you say, how you act, how you respond in certain situations, how you interact with others at work, at play, even at home or on social media, all contributes to the *Perceptional Messaging* others will receive. But here's the good news: you are the transmitter and, as such, you can control the perceptional messages you want released; and, more importantly, you can control how they are perceived!

Jeff Olson, a mentor, colleague, entrepreneur, speaker and successful author, wrote a wonderful book called *The Slight Edge*. In his book, he literally nails the difference between successful and unsuccessful people. He asks the reader: "What do successful people do, that the unsuccessful don't?" Most people will try to answer that question with one big, ultimate answer. They want the secret ingredient, the golden key, the magic potion to drink that will bring success flowing into their lives. Unfortunately, that's not how it works. But we live in a world where we want instant gratification. We want what we want right now! It's why the lottery is so popular. It's why Netflix, Hulu and Amazon have begun to replace standard television and even cable TV. It's why, with the click of a button, you can announce to all your "friends" on Facebook you just broke your leg, and then sit back and watch all the sympathy, prayers and warm thoughts come flooding in to help lift your spirits … But that's not the secret.

Jeff Olson teaches that it's not the big things, or that one big task or event that makes a difference. It's the little things. It's the little things that you do each and every day that, at the time of doing them, seem to have little to no impact on your success. However, *those little things compounded over time can and will have a huge impact!* To better explain, Jeff uses a lunch analogy that goes something like this: Let's say today you and I went to lunch. I ordered a salad, and you ordered a fat, juicy cheese burger. Now at that point in time, am I any healthier than you because I ate a single salad, and you ate a fat, greasy cheese burger? Of course not. But compounded over time, three months, six months, even six years, your choice of food can surely have an impact! That, my friend, is The Slight Edge. The secret to success is so slight, most people miss it, and it's right in front of you. If you read only ten pages of a business book today, are you all of a sudden a Master of Business? No. But how about ten pages a day for a year? That's 3,650 pages, or an average of about fifteen books in a year! Do you think that will have a positive impact on your career? Absolutely!

With that in mind, now let's talk about perception. What is *Perceptional Messaging*? *Perceptional Messaging* is: The subtle art of influencing how one is perceived by others, through intentional and strategic actions. There are six areas of *Perceptional Messaging* to master both during and outside of work, that we will discuss in the next two chapters. Remember, none of what we are about to discuss individually will have a huge impact immediately. However, compounded over time these little perceptional messages will make a big difference. It's the *slight edge* of business that, compounded over time, will have a huge impact on your success. *Perceptional Messaging* is one of the well-hidden secrets of *The Executive Arena*, and an integral part of gaining the advantage in corporate politics. It's a skill you must master, and a very powerful weapon if you implement it. Let's discuss the six areas of *Perceptional Messaging* in detail.

1. Dress/Appearance:

Most people will look their very best during the initial job interview. As the old saying goes, you "dress to impress" throughout the process. Unfortunately, once the interview is over, most if not all of us let our guard down. We decide to blend in with the environment/culture of the workplace, so we feel accepted more quickly. We have to become part of the team. When in Rome we need to do what the Romans do, right? Well, not exactly; not if you want to project a positive or *slightly higher* perceptional message than everyone else. *That's the key* when it comes to our appearance: dress *better (if even slightly) than everyone else.*

I'm not saying to overdress by wearing a tux in a shorts and flip-flops environment. In fact, just the opposite. Even a three-piece suit would be going overboard in that situation. The last thing you want to do is to look like you're over dressing *on purpose.* So, whatever the working environment calls for, i.e., casual or business casual, step it up a notch. If you are allowed to wear jeans, wear jeans with perhaps an untucked dress shirt and tie. Or, instead of jeans, wear dress slacks and a polo shirt. And pay attention to your shoes! I mean this for both men and women. Believe it or not, dress shoes or heels can look pretty sharp with a pair of jeans, so don't be afraid to try it. It can make a big difference when compared to tennis shoes, sandals or flip-flops.

Your appearance is not just about what clothes you are wearing. Your grooming standards are also extremely important. Let's be honest, we have all been lazy a time or two in the morning and didn't shave, or didn't put on makeup that day because we were "tired" or "didn't have time" or "will be traveling all day, no one will see me." There is no excuse for not looking your best. Aside from the obvious fact that looking good makes you feel good, and thus gives you a boost of extra energy, it's one surefire way to make you stand out. By looking your best, day after day, over time you project the perceptional message that, "You've got things together." "She's always prepared and ready to go, regardless of the situation." "He always looks sharp." So, do your hair, brush your teeth, shave, put on the makeup and, yes, it's okay to smell nice. Just don't overdo it. It's okay if you sit next to someone, and they can smell your cologne or perfume. It's not okay if they can smell you from across the executive boardroom or, worse, from the other side of the parking lot.

Let's look at the big picture from another angle:

> **Executive Arena Rule:** If you can't manage your time each and every day to ensure you look your best, or if you don't care enough to manage your own image, how do you expect to be trusted to manage a company or manage its image?

If you think that statement is a little inflated or farfetched, it's not. If you don't believe people sometimes actually think that way of others, think again. The perceptional messages you project can be positive or negative. The choice is up to you. In summary, *dress and act at the level you aspire to.*

2. Your Space/Environment:

Next, you need to be aware of the environment around you that you can control. While this still relates to your appearance, it warrants its own section. What else in your day-to-day life will give off a positive or negative message? What else do you have control over?

Office: Let's start with your office or workspace. I don't care how many people say a sloppy desk is a sign of genius. Einstein wasn't looking to make a six-figure salary or run a company. When it comes to your workspace, even if you only have a small desk or cubicle right now, the condition of your workspace is a sign of organization or lack thereof. It's an extension of you. You may actually be one of the most organized people in the world, but what perceptional message is your workspace sending out? What is it saying about you? So keep it tidy! Keep some furniture polish and other cleaning supplies on hand and get some organizational bins if you need them. And remember, everything has its place. Bring in a couple family pictures so those around you know family is important to you. Perceptional message? Work/life balance. Perhaps get yourself a desk calendar. The large ones that almost act like a large placemat. While most of us use Outlook or similar for keeping our schedules, the desk calendar gleams *organization*. You don't even have to write on it, just get one. It's also good for keeping coffee and food stains off your desk, and each month you get to tear off the old month and start with a fresh new sheet! It's a disposable table cloth.

Your Car: Another area that is often neglected or thought to be irrelevant is your car. Yes, the vehicle you drive. I'm not taking about the *kind* of car or how expensive it is, though that can be a factor. I'm talking about its condition. The week-old McDonalds bags in the back seat. The dog- or cat-hair-filled floor mats, or the windows that are so dirty you can write your name on them. I'm talking about the weeks, or even months, of junk mail you tossed on the floor, that has now grown into a mountain-like structure.

Believe it or not, the condition of your vehicle has more perceptional value than the actual type of car you drive. So keep it clean, inside and out. I've had many employees give me lifts to and from the airport or dinner throughout my career. Case in point, I was more impressed with the spotless and well-cared-for Dodge Minivan than I was with the filthy, "something smells in here" BMW. Just like your workspace, your vehicle is an extension of you and thus, so is its condition. It also shows that you take pride in and will care for things of value. Not a bad trait for an aspiring executive to have, don't you think?

Smoking: Finally, and this is a big one ... smoking. I have been a smoker almost my entire life, and just recently (about two years ago) I gave it up for good. I can tell you without a shadow of a doubt that smoking can and does have a negative impact on your career. I'm not talking about the obvious health issues related to smoking. I'm talking once again about your image and the *perceptional message* others receive. Let's be honest. If you smoke, I assure you others *will* be offended or, at the very least, turned off if they are a non-smoker. God help you if they are an ex-smoker. Ex-smokers are even less tolerant, though I can't tell you why. Back in the days of *Mad Men*—loved that show—which was not very long ago, there was an ashtray in every office, airport terminal and hallway. In fact, the only place you'd see a no-smoking sign was in an elevator or hospital. It's funny how you still see those no-smoking signs in elevators today, even though there is no smoking in the entire building. Back then it was "cool" to smoke, especially in the corporate environment. It was an acceptable, almost welcomed practice. However, things have changed, drastically. As of 2015, according to the CDC, less than 16% of the US population smokes and it's declining every year. That means about 85% of Americans do not smoke! So, if you whip out that smoke at a company function, or walk around smelling like an ashtray, rest assured you could turn off about 85% of those around you. I'm not a gambling man, but if I'm trying to improve my image, puffing away on that cig is not helping my cause.

That said, I know not everyone can quit, nor does everyone *want* to quit. I loved smoking, and, from time to time, I still get those urges to smoke. If you absolutely must smoke, then, at the very least, do your best to hide it. Make it your "little secret." The fact that you are even trying to keep it a secret puts a positive spin on your nasty little habit. I remember years ago coming back in from having a smoke, and a colleague asked, "Did you leave to just put on some fresh cologne?"

"No, I stepped out for a smoke, and didn't want to smell like an ashtray," I answered.

They thanked me genuinely with a smile. In that situation the perceptional message turned from "I don't really care about my health or those around me" to "I respect those around me. I know I have a bad habit and I'm working on it." See the drastic difference in the perceptional message? So try to keep it away from others. I knew a colleague who would keep a bottle of Febreze just outside the back door of the building. When she finished smoking, she would spray herself to try to mask the smell of cigarettes and pop a piece of gum in her mouth before she came back inside. Another friend of mine would use an electronic (odorless) cigarette while at work, never smoking the real thing during working hours. There are many ways not to offend, so get creative and do what you have to do. It *will* make a difference.

3. Emails:

These are the best of times, these are the worst of times. Not quite the quote from *A Tale of Two Cities*, but still very relevant today in relation to that wonderful invention called email. What started out as just another business tool to aid in communication has now become the single most important medium used in business today. In fact, aside from the occasional business meeting, it's completely safe to say businesses are now run and managed in large part through email. I have personally witnessed long email chains between two people who were no more than fifty feet apart. Whether a few cubicles away from each other or offices directly across the hall from one another, people today choose to use email instead of getting off their butt and having a face-to-face conversation. Regardless of the pros and cons of email, it's here to stay. And, as such, you must know when and how to use it properly, to ensure the perceptional messages you are sending are advantageous to your career.

In the workplace, it becomes very easy to "say what you feel" when you are responding to or sending an email. Being able to hide behind that computer screen of yours and express your feelings can be quite easy when you don't have to physically face the person you are communicating with. Even worse, everything you say in an email is now *in writing!* Forever! It's now in a physical form, "on the record," and can be copied, saved and forwarded to anyone. Have you ever known someone who used to send horrible, unprofessional emails at work? Are they still with the company? The point is, professional opinions are being formed of you in large part by the way you communicate, and in today's world that includes email as a major medium. So here are some critical email rules to ensure your *Perceptional Messaging* remains advantageous to your career.

1. *Do not* have "conversations" through email. If you are about to send an email to a single individual that will result in more than one or two replies back and forth, then pick up a phone, or go talk face to face. Anything more than a couple emails is a conversation, and it's more meaningful to just talk, using your voice, to the person directly. In *The Executive Arena, direct verbal communication always trumps email!* It builds relationships and trust and, most importantly, you can ensure the message you are sending is being perceived correctly. While emojis are becoming more and more popular to assist with the feeling of a message, they will never replace the emotional benefits of human interaction.

2. *Do not* use email when you're upset. If you receive a mean, nasty or otherwise unprofessional email, or one that just gets you angry or upset, *do not* respond. We all have that natural "How dare you say that? Let me tell you something!" tendency, but I assure you it's the wrong thing to do. The last thing you want to do is bring yourself down to the unprofessional level of the person who sent the email. Instead, take a deep breath and calm down before responding. If possible, wait until the next day if it was that upsetting. It's bad enough sending an angry email, let alone getting into a heated argument through email, especially one that has others copied in the chain. Simply not responding sends a more professional message than trying to *one up* or *state your case* to the sender. Just walk away and address the email at a later time. If the situation warrants, use rule number one

and go talk to the person directly. Trust me, if the sender learns you are going to confront them directly each time you get an unprofessional email, they just might rethink sending it the next time.

3. *Do not* use email if they are nearby. Aside from the walls being in the way, if you can hit the person with a tennis ball, go talk to them instead of using email. Of course, there are always times when you must use email. Sending or requesting documents, giving someone a reminder, notifying multiple parties of a situation, or anytime you need a record of the communication. The list goes on and on. We both can agree email is great and I can't even imagine life without it. But imagine the impact if you could just increase your human interactions by 10%. Getting more personal, more face-time with the people you work with, regardless of how limited or short the conversation, is extremely valuable in *The Executive Arena*. Again, it's shipbuilding. Why do you think golf is so popular among executives? It's the only sport where you can actually have a meaningful conversation, and even talk business while playing it. We will discuss golf in detail in a later chapter. So, get off your butt and have a conversation and a smile.

4. *Do not* respond to emails while under the influence or extremely tired. I know this should go without saying, but I have to say it anyway. If you have had a few drinks, *do not* respond to emails. We, including myself, have all done it, and it's wrong. Even if you've only had two drinks, alcohol does affect your thought process, and you will not be at your best. The same goes if you are extremely tired. If you have had a long day, and are finally at home resting on the couch, do *not* get involved with answering

emails. It's okay to check emails, and maybe send the occasional "I'll get that to you in the morning." But unless you are at your best, don't bother taking on any situation that will require your undivided attention. It's okay to put the phone down, to close your laptop and wait until tomorrow. Notice I said *do not* respond to emails if you are under the influence or tired. I didn't say never check your emails after hours. In fact, checking and answering emails after hours is a great way to project that you are always on the ball and care about the company. One of the best perceptional messages you can ever send out to the powers that be is "I'm always working," especially when it's late into the night. Just don't do it if you are not at your best.

5. *Increase your writing ability!* Since a good percentage of your communication at work is through email, you *must* be a decent writer, or at least be able to cheat until you can improve. By cheat I mean use spellcheck and grammar checker *before* you hit the *send* button. Let's face it, we live in a world now where writing is important. Back in 2012, *The Huffington Post* reported that 85% of the world was connected by email, and that study was done over six years ago, so the percentage is much higher now. When was the last time you wrote (hand wrote) and mailed (via USPS) a letter to someone? I hear some of you saying never!

Thanks to advanced word processing software like Microsoft Word and Apple Pages, there is no excuse for releasing any kind of written word into the public (or at work) that reads like crap. Have you ever received a résumé that was filled with all kinds of misspelled words and grammatical errors?

What were your first impressions of that candidate? Not very good I would expect. I've seen posts on Facebook, LinkedIn, even emails at work, that consisted of one hundred words in a single sentence! No periods, capitalization, nothing. If that doesn't scream "I don't care" then it surely screams "I don't know how to write a coherent sentence." The written communications you send out every day should read as if you take pride in their construction. Take an extra few seconds before you hit the *send* button and review your message. Make sure spell check is set to *automatic* in your settings and use the tools at your disposal to ensure your emails are the best they can be. Remember, in almost every management description it reads "effective communicator" as a requirement.

> **Executive Arena Rule:** When you are an aspiring executive, the interview never ends.

The good news is you don't have to go back to school to improve your writing ability. Start reading the newspaper or magazines (even electronically). Read articles or blogs that interest you. Take a creative writing class, write a book or white paper, or just start writing for practice. Read and write about anything you like, but *write*! The more you read and write the better you will become. The old saying still applies: "Practice makes perfect."

Points to Remember:

1. You must learn that everything you do, everything you say, how you act, how you respond in certain situations, how you interact with others at work, at play, even at home or on social media, all contributes to the perceptional message others will receive.

2. Others' perceptions of you is *half* the battle. In other words, even your exceptional work performance will only account for about 50% of your success!

3. *Always* dress for success! Put on the makeup, shave, slap on the tie, keep your car clean, and your desk/office workspace organized. Everyone is watching!

4. Though a picture is worth a thousand words, a bad email has ruined thousands of careers. Be careful of the message (no pun intended) you are sending out into the world of bits and bytes. Once released, you can't take it back.

Chapter Four: *Perceptional Messaging - at Home*

Michael stood at the front of the class, ready to begin the next team-building exercise. The standard paper tents were filled out with the names of each attendee and placed neatly in front of them on the desks. Michael silently glanced over those in attendance, scanning and mentally noting the vast physical and cultural differences among his students. Black, white, male, female, young and old. The pool of GMs (general managers) at the company was very diverse. This can make it difficult for any leadership consultant to connect with the group, let alone for them to connect with each other, but I had faith. If anyone could do it, Michael could. I had hired Michael to do a two-day session at our annual management retreat and conference we were holding in Las Vegas. I had all the GMs fly in for four days to provide them some solid sales and leadership training, as well as provide a formal setting to share best practices from around the country. I had recently been promoted to vice president and, with the actual president, CEO and both owners/founders of the company in attendance, this had to go off well for *my* career's sake. No pressure.

I had known Michael for many years as I had been through many of his sales/leadership training sessions at a previous company. His message and teaching style really hit home with me, and I became a raving fan of his teachings very early in my career. I attributed a good portion of my success to Michael's teachings. Now in senior management myself, I was hoping Michael would have the same effect on others as he did on me when I was starting my management career.

I had chosen Vegas, again because of what I had learned from Michael long ago. No, it had nothing to do with "what happens in Vegas, stays in Vegas." It had everything to do with employees being offsite, away from work. If you want to build a cohesive team of members that are normally geographically separate from each other, don't do it at a work location. I have seen many companies decide to fly in their sales teams, GMs, executives—whatever—for an annual meeting, and instead of doing it at a neutral location, they do it at a company-owned location. Seriously? If you really want to instill out-of-the-box thinking, creative thoughts and ideas, and promote an open-minded atmosphere, never ever do it on location, or, even worse, at the corporate headquarters. Doing so will only ensure everyone is on their best behavior. That's not a bad thing, but, rest assured, that's likely all you'll get: good behavior.

Some will tell you, "We did it this way to save on expenses." That's a bunch of bull crap. Everyone is already in a hotel, has a rental car, has paid for their flight etc. Those expenses don't change. Rent a conference room at a nearby hotel, close to the corporate office if need be. With all the rooms you are renting, you may even get the conference room for free, or at least at a discount. Getting people out of their element is the best way to see their true colors, and it opens the door for genuine learning and growth, and fosters creative ideas. I'll get off my soap box now.

I welcomed everyone and thanked them for coming—as if they had a choice—then proudly introduced Michael. I made sure I included Michael's accolades and accomplishments to boost his credibility to the team, and Michael did the same for me after he thanked me for "allowing him this opportunity to work with such professionals." He was great at giving compliments without seeming to do so.

To break the ice, Michael asked that, one at a time, each person stand up and provide everyone with a few facts about themselves. Those fact would be:

1. Your name.
2. Where you are from. (In other words, born and raised, not what location you manage.)
3. What location you manage. (Of course.)
4. How long you have been with the company.
5. Then the kicker: What one significant event in your life thus far has made you or helped make you the person you are today?

The last question is a great one, if you don't give people a lot of time to think about their answer. The responses were awesome! Everything from delivering my first child to getting married to living overseas. I was amazed how much the team was sharing with each other, and pleasantly surprised that most of their best moments were events that happened in their private lives. I loved it! Then it was Carol's turn. When Michael handed her the floor to answer her five questions, she answered the first four, and then said, "As for number five, no thanks." Michael, thinking she was kidding, chuckled and replied, "It's okay, we don't bite. Please continue." To our surprise, in a serious voice she responded, "I don't share my personal life at work." Wow, talk about *Perceptional Messaging*!

Silence filled the room for what I'm sure was only a second or two, though it felt like forever. The president and I locked eyes for a moment as we both exchanged WTF glances. Michael, not missing a beat, as though he had been through this before, said, "Fair enough," dismissing her with a slow blink and nod. He turned his head right, looked to the gentleman next to her and, with a smile, said, "Brad? You're next. The floor is yours."

Carol's reason for not playing nice is irrelevant. The fact that she announced her negative attitude to the entire class, in a very disrespectful way, spoke volumes. Now, you may agree somewhat with Carol and think to yourself that no one has to share their personal life with anyone. And you're right! They don't have to, and it's well within their rights not to. But this book isn't about rights, is it? The perceptual message Carol sent out to all in attendance did not help her career in the slightest. In fact, I'd rank that situation as a CLM, or what is commonly known in *The Executive Arena* as a *Career Limiting Move*. Regardless of her true reasons or intentions, Carol sent out a list of perceptional messages in one shot that were somewhere in the ballpark of: *I don't like the class we're in, I don't like this company, I don't care for the people I work for, I'm embarrassed by my personal life, I'm better than all of you, my personal life sucks, I don't have it together,* etc. etc. The list goes on and on, depending on the receiver, but you get the point. There was nothing good going to come from such a display. Unfortunately, her employment lasted roughly two more months before she was put on performance probation and eventually terminated.

The moral of this story is: you can and sometimes should share pieces of your personal life with those you work with. It can definitely help you build trust and strengthen relationships. Again, this falls into the shipbuilding category. Its tells everyone you're human, just as they are. It's good to let people know you are more than just the boss, or that you have a family to support, or that the job you have is important to you. That said, please take notice. I said it's okay to share "pieces" of your personal life, *not* everything.

Just as you are on your best behavior while at work, so should you be while away from work. Or, at the very least, control what others will perceive about your life away from work. Have you ever noticed that most presidents or CEOs vary rarely show up to an after-work company function? Or, in the rare case they do, it's very brief and they simply make an appearance and then leave. And for very good reason. They have an image to uphold. Wait, what? They have an image to uphold? You mean they want to ensure the perceptions others have of them are always professional, even positive? I sense things are really starting to sink in. So, let's get right into our next topic: *Perceptional Messaging* from home.

1. Social Media:

What started out as small private chatrooms on such platforms as AOL and Myspace has now grown into a billion-dollar industry with such giants as Facebook, Twitter, Pinterest, LinkedIn, and Snapchat, just to name a few. You can read blogs, join groups, share your interests, your lifestyle, even advertise to the entire world your every step while on a family vacation. You can share what you're doing, where you've been, and where you're going next. It's all there for you to use and, for the most part, it's all free! However, just as you need to control the perceptional messages you send out at work, you need to control them on social media. I'm not saying not to use Facebook, for example. I use Facebook and love the way I can keep up with old friends and family in ways never heard of fifteen years ago. But, make no mistake, everyone is watching, so you need to keep a handle on what you are putting out to the world. More importantly to your current and future employers! I use Facebook for personal, and LinkedIn for business. Here are a few critical things you need to remember if you are to use social media.

a. *Unprofessional Moments*: We've all had them. The nasty post, the drunk party you attended, the embarrassing picture, even the argument you had online with someone. It's critical these kinds of situations do *not* make it back to the eyes of your employer or even a coworker. My wife is a senior manager in human resources and I can tell you with certainty, some employers look up potential or even current employees on social media sites, and will even do Google searches to see if anything negative pops up! So be mindful of what you are posting and, most importantly, what *friend requests* you accept from someone at work. My suggestion is *do not* become *friends* with a current coworker on Facebook or other "personal" type sites. Use LinkedIn to connect with business colleagues. We will talk about the importance of LinkedIn in a few moments.

b. *Pictures* they *take*: While you may be very diligent in monitoring your social media posts, don't forget about the pictures your "friends" may take and post on their page. If you are out and about, at a gathering, etc., be aware of the multiple cell phones in the hands of just about everyone around you. All too often I have seen the not-so-flattering pic make it back to a current employer. The perceptional message was not positive.

c. *Politics*: *Never ever, ever* comment, share, like, or otherwise post your political views on social media. I don't care how strongly you feel about a subject, candidate, political party or sitting president, *do not* talk politics on social media. It's just too big a risk that you will offend or, most likely (in today's world), piss someone off. Once again you may be saying, "But this is America. I have free speech and my views should not affect my career goals or what someone thinks of me." I'm here to be a little in your face and tell you, once again, this book is not about your rights or freedoms. Of course you have the right to say whatever you want, but just because you have the right to do something, doesn't mean it's the right thing to do in relation to your career. So, go ahead and post away about how you don't like President Trump, or how you think Hillary Clinton is a crook. Just remember this: your boss or someone else of influence at work may have a completely different view. And unlike race, religion or age, your *political view* is not a protected class. Get the picture?

d. *Professional and Private*: I think we can all agree: social media is a way of life now and it's here to stay. Just as with the advent of email, or smartphones, we must all learn to embrace these changes and utilize them to our advantage. Simply rejecting or refusing to use this new technology will only hinder your career and limit the wonderful tools at your disposal. So, how do we manage social media effectively, not only to protect us from negative exposure, but to use it to our advantage and advance our career? The answer is simple: multiple accounts! In other words, separate your *personal* from your *business*. I don't mean have two Facebook accounts. I'm talking about using certain social media platforms for your personal and business needs. I use Facebook only for my friends and family, and very rarely do I have a work colleague as a "friend" on Facebook. There are some ex-coworkers that are now friends of mine on Facebook, but the key word here is "ex." For business I like to use LinkedIn. LinkedIn is mainly used for business networking and can come in very handy when it comes to connecting with others in your industry and around the world. There are other platforms coming online, most recently "Alignable," which is mainly for business networking with a local feel. You should choose one that feels right for you and your career and stay active, reading, liking and sharing posts from other business professionals.

2. Your Personal Life:

As you may remember, Carol, as we discussed earlier, was reluctant to share her personal life with her coworkers and, as we learned, she did so to her dismay. So you may be asking: Just how much or little of my personal life should I share?

Well, honestly, the answer is really quite simple: share the positive, avoid the negative. Remember, in *The Executive Arena* it's also about *shipbuilding*: connecting with others and building relationships, mentorships, and partnerships! So it's okay to share the news that you're attending your brother's wedding this weekend, or that you're pregnant with your second child. When you are informing your employees that you will be out of the office on Friday, it's okay to tell them it's your tenth wedding anniversary. Sharing that you volunteer at a soup kitchen once a month, or that you coach a little league team, or you tutor kids in math is wonderful! You see, sharing personal information like this lets those around you know that you do have a life outside the office. But, more importantly, the perceptional message you are sending is: "I care about you, I trust you, and I don't mind sharing with you some personal things that mean a lot to me." A message like that will pay huge dividends when it comes to building loyalty with subordinates, coworkers, and even your superiors.

That said, it's important to note you should stay away from anything that could be considered a negative. Remember, it's the receiver's perception that matters, not yours. Don't talk about your brother who's an alcoholic, or that you're going to court because your neighbor filed a lawsuit against you. Don't ever speak ill of your spouse or significant other, even in joking, regardless of how petty or insignificant you may think it is. I remember a colleague stating he "loves his wife, but she's a slob and doesn't believe in cleaning, so their house is always a mess." What do you think the first impressions were when she was finally introduced at a company function? Better yet, is it safe to assume from his statement that *he* doesn't help with the housework, and expects the *woman* to clean the house? You see, interpretations can vary widely, so it's just not worth the risk to share anything of a negative nature. I don't care who you are speaking with, or the situation, don't do it. If you need to take time off work for a problem that might be considered "negative," then simply state it's for personal reasons, or that you have family matters to attend to. Being short in your reason is better than sharing the negative. Attending to family matters is always a respected reason for time off in business.

3. Your Health:

When we speak of someone's health, we normally mean both physical and mental. It's no secret that a strong body builds a strong mind, and thus if one is to become successful in the corporate world, one must absolutely be healthy, or constantly working towards being healthy. However, in *The Executive Arena*, the world of corporate politics, it's actually more important to be constantly striving towards better health, even if you feel you're in pretty good health. In other words, I'm once again talking about the perceptional message you are sending or should be sending on a constant basis. Yes, it's extremely important you exercise, eat right, and maintain a healthy, active lifestyle. But it's just as important to let the people around you know you are doing just that. Let me put it this way. Let's say there are three people in your office that you work with. The first is a slender man who seems to be in good health because he obviously doesn't struggle with his weight. We've all met the type. They are the ones that can eat a horse, and the only one gaining weight is the person sitting closest to them. Second is the overweight gentleman who brings his own large bags of snacks to the office to keep a good supply of carbs and sugar flowing into his system. He's simply a nice guy who loves to eat, right? Lastly is the woman who's slightly, if barely, overweight but is actually involved in a healthy routine. She has a gym membership and uses it every day for forty-five minutes after work. She has a protein shake for lunch, followed by a brisk walk around the parking lot, instead of heading to the company cafeteria for some greasy food and drama talk. She is slowly losing weight and toning, and every day inches one step closer to her personal goal. Let's assume each of them have the same qualifications, the same experience and company tenure. Which would you choose to head up your new department? It all falls back to what I said in a previous chapter. If someone can't manage themselves, how can they be trusted to manage a department or company? If you think you don't need to improve, how can you grow personally or professionally? And, if you can't grow, how do you expect to be trusted to grow the company? Do you see where I'm coming from here? It's all about what others perceive!

I hope by now you to realize the true and ultimate power of *Perceptional Messaging*. The term "act as if" still rings true and has a lot of validity, but, as you now understand, there is a much deeper meaning. The *perceptions others have of you* are so important, and *more* than half the battle. You must learn to manage the perceptional messages you are sending out to the world, including controlling how these messages are perceived to ensure they are beneficial to *your* goals. Control this, manage this, master this element of *Corporate Political Intelligence* and you are well on your way to controlling your own destiny.

Points to Remember:

1. Share the positive situations of your personal life with others you work with. It reminds them you are human too and helps to build communication and loyalty among your subordinates, peers and superiors.
2. Avoid sharing the negative situations of your personal life, and never, ever speak ill about your spouse or significant other, or a family member, regardless of the situation.
3. Begin to consistently focus on your health, both physically and mentally. The one who believes in consistently improving their own health surely believes in consistent company growth and improvement.

Chapter Five: Fishing off the Company
Pier - *Mixing business and pleasure.*

Part One - Office hook-ups

"Excuse me," she said as she tapped my shoulder. I turned around to find a smiling, bright and extremely good-looking woman, standing next to her friend, staring back at me. "I just wanted to say," she continued, "that I really enjoyed your class. You're a really good instructor." As I recall, I believe I at least said thank you as she walked out of my class. Honestly, I don't remember what I said, but I do know that I was in awe. So much that to this day I couldn't tell you who her friend was or how she might have looked. All I know was that I was immediately attracted to her. I went to the classroom doorway and nonchalantly peaked around the corner and watched as she and her friend walked further and further away, still giggling and smiling as they did while I was teaching.

At that time, I was a senior instructor and training supervisor for a computer training company in downtown Chicago. It was the first job after my honorable discharge from the navy that I truly enjoyed. Being a previous naval instructor, and loving computers in general, the job was a perfect match for me.

Wanting to know a little more about her, I went back into the classroom to look at the little name tents the students left on their desks. These were little cardboard name plates we had each student fill out, fold in half, and place on their desks before class began. It helped us connect with each student on a personal level, as we were able to call on each student by name.

Her name was Sharon and, after further investigation, I realized she was not just a student in my class, she was an employee of the company. She was a new instructor assigned to audit my class as all new instructors were required to do as part of their initial instructor qualifications. This was great news to me! It had been over a year since I left my last relationship and I had not been on any dates up until this point. Honestly, I was not serious about getting involved again until my career was on track. But this was different. I wanted to find out more about her and what she was all about. I needed to get to know her, but I didn't want to mess things up. I wanted to do it right. I, of course, was her supervisor, so how could I possibly get to know her on a personal level without jeopardizing my career or hers? Then it came to me. I'd go to my boss first! Just hear me out on this.

Bob was originally from southern California and was recently assigned as the new general manager of the Chicago location. He had been on board for about six months and was diligently working on turning around our location from a performance standpoint. While he was not my direct supervisor, I felt comfortable going directly to Bob as we seemed to hit things off right from the start. I mean, come on, I wasn't actually going to him for anything work related anyway; not directly related. Additionally, if you recall Chapter Two where we discussed *Knowing the Players and How They Move*, I knew Bob was a mentor. He took pride in coaching and giving advice to those in his charge. He was just the person I needed to talk to.

"Hey Bob," I greeted as I walked into his office. He always kept his door open unless he was having an extremely private conversation. "Do you have a minute?"

Bob looked up quickly to see who was seeking his attention. "Hey, Richard! Sure. Sit down," he replied, as his gaze went back to intently staring at his laptop. I could tell by the look on his face he was working diligently on something important to him, but I really needed his help. So I sat down and gently spoke the words that I knew were magical to a mentor. "I need your advice about something important," I stated firmly. Bob closed his laptop, leaned back in his chair, turned his body slightly to face directly towards me, crossed his arms on his chest and replied, "What's up?" I had his full attention.

"Well, I need to know if there are any company policies against dating other employees?" I asked very matter-of-factly.

Bob, trying not to smile, scrunched his eyebrows and asked in a very slow and curious voice, "And you are asking this because ...?"

"Well," I began to explain, "there was this new instructor auditing my class today, and, frankly, I would like to ask her out on a date. I just wasn't sure if it was against company policy or not?"

Bob was not only a master at *Corporate Political Intelligence*, he was also a master at releasing the tension in the room. "Is she cute?" he asked with a big smile from ear to ear, knowing it would embarrass me.

"Yes, she's cute," I said abruptly, beginning to regret coming to Bob for help in the first place.

Bob could see the redness of my face, and now satisfied he'd had his little fun with me, gave me the answer I was hoping for. "Well, there are no official policies about dating employees," he explained. "I mean, let's face it, the company even buys booze once a month on a Friday for the employees, so it's clear they are not too concerned with any sort of liability."

"That's good to know," I quickly injected. "So, you don't have an issue with employees dating?" I asked again for clarification.

"Well, while there is no company policy against this," Bob explained, "you are her supervisor. However, as long as it doesn't affect your performance, or hers, I'm totally fine with it. You have my blessing."

At that point we both smiled and Bob, believing the conversation was over, went back to the laptop project he was working on before my arrival.

"Can I get that in writing?" I asked with the most serious face I could possibly muster at that moment. It wasn't working.

"Let me get this straight," Bob exclaimed as he once again looked up at me. "You want me to write a letter stating it's okay for you to date someone, who doesn't even know you like them yet, and may actually turn you down?"

"Yes, please," I replied, while realizing how foolish the request actually sounded. Holding my ground and waiting for a response, I continued looking down at the floor, contemplating whether life on this planet would ever get better.

After a short pause that seemed like forever, Bob, with a you-owe-me-one look and a warm smile of approval said, "Give me until the end of the day. I'll have a letter typed up for you." "On company letterhead"? I asked with a cringe. The glance that followed was enough to tell me it was time to go, quickly! So I did.

Now armed with a letter from the general manager, I was ready to ask her out. I had permission, she obviously knew who I was and she already had respect for me from a business standpoint, so what was the hold up? God only knows. I was so nervous it took me a few days to muster up the courage and to find the perfect time to approach her. Finally, I caught up with her in the instructors' lounge. It was a small room the size of a master bedroom closet, with no windows and about five computers to practice our lessons on. She was getting ready to teach a new class and needed some "prep time," as they called it, to prepare.

I sat up on the counter, my feet barely touching the floor, with my legs swaying back and forth. "So, I was thinking," I began to mumble. "I was wondering if you'd like to maybe go out sometime? Maybe, perhaps some dinner or something?" Whew! There, I said it! I did it! But her response wasn't what I was expecting. Honestly, I was expecting (or at least prepared for) "no thanks," or "not right now"; anything but what followed.

"Well, you are my supervisor," she responded, "so don't you think that's a little unethical?"

I'm not sure how, to this day, it actually played out so perfectly, but, without missing a beat, I responded, "Not at all. I actually have this …" and immediately pulled the folded-up approval letter from my pocket and handed it to her.

With a puzzled look, she took it from my hands and slowly unfolded the letter. I could see a slight smile forming on her face as she read the beautifully crafted permission slip. Come on, how could she say no? She didn't.

Fast forward to today, as I am writing this book, Sharon and I just celebrated our twentieth wedding anniversary, gratefully looking forward to the next twenty years being even better than the first. Luckily things worked out for the better.

The topic of this chapter could have easily been included in the previous chapter about *Perceptional Messaging*. However, I thought it important enough to have its own chapter, so you may understand the seriousness of mixing business and pleasure, or what I call, *fishing off the company pier*. Please understand that my story, while 100% true, is the exception, not the rule! Workplace romances almost 90% of the time do *not* have happy endings. In fact, most lead to accusations of inappropriate behavior, sexual harassment charges, favoritism and other company policy infractions, many of which have led to job loss. Even worse, not only do most work relationships end badly, so have many careers in the aftermath of what should have never taken place. And this doesn't even include situations that involve a senior executive or any superior/subordinate situation.

Vault Careers does their Office Romance Survey every year and in 2016 reported that, of the people surveyed, 22% of men and 15% of women admitted to having some sort of random workplace hookup. One could argue the figures are actually much higher because not everyone will admit to it, even on a survey. However, not surprisingly, less that 10% of either gender met their spouse or life partner at work. The report said that the majority of respondents don't have a problem with relationships between colleagues in principle. However, many believe that some rules should apply. The most common "unacceptable" romances were: coworkers at different levels (33%); those who work on projects together (30%); and those who work in the same department (24%). At the other end of the scale, just 6% of respondents believe that workplace romances are never acceptable. So only a very small number actually think it's wrong! Are you getting the picture? Knowing these numbers, I want you to consider the following. There's an old saying: "If only 5% are extremely successful, why follow the other 95%?" In other words, if you want to be successful in business, do what the successful people do. Don't follow the majority. Just because most people love cheeseburgers doesn't mean they are good for you. This should ring true here when it comes to office hookups. Believe it or not, from the same Vault report, of those who actually admitted to having a fling, 71% of the men said they would do it again, while 57% of woman said they would as well.

When I first read these statistics, I was floored, but the more I thought about it, the more it all made sense. Any company, regardless of the industry, has more frontline employees than it does senior executives. Just like a pyramid, the higher you rise in a company the fewer the like positions. There are more general employees than there are supervisors. There are more supervisors than there are managers. There are more managers than there are directors, and so on up to the president and/or CEO. Don't get me wrong. I'm not saying that people in management positions don't have office flings. They do to the same *percentage* as the rest, but remember there are fewer of them because of fewer base numbers. In other words, the really successful people in any company account for only about 5% of the employee total.

In summary, the odds of anything good coming from an office fling, at any level, are slim to none. Just don't do it!

Finally, if you are wondering if certain industries have a higher percentage of office romances, then check this out, compliments of Vault Careers once again. The hospitality and tourism industry ranked #1 among office romances, with 61% of employees saying they've had some kind of workplace relationship. I mean, hello ... Hotels and resorts? That places them ahead of consumer products (59%), retail and advertising (both at 58%), government (54%, no surprise there), human resources (53%) and technology (51%). Did you catch that? Human resources at 53%? I'll wait while you let that sink in.

Part Two - Other ways to fish

Aside from the previously stated and obvious office flings, there are many other things you will want to avoid when it comes to using the "company pier." Mixing business and pleasure has a much broader meaning in *The Executive Arena* than it does in the traditional sense. There are situations you should avoid or limit to the best of your ability if you are to flourish and achieve your career goals.

Financial dealings: "Neither a borrower nor a lender be." (William Shakespeare)

Whether it's buying a car, or borrowing $20, never be the borrower or lender, buyer or seller in any transaction with a subordinate or direct report. I would venture to say, don't do it with coworkers either as it's simply not worth the risk.

Back in 1986 I was living in Jacksonville, Florida, stationed on the USS *Forrestal*, CV-59, an aircraft carrier out of Mayport Naval Station. I had been in the navy almost four years and had heard that my supervisor—we will call him Bruce—needed a place to stay. I decided to rent him a room at my place since, even at just twenty-two years old, I owned my own home and could use the extra cash for bills. Hey, I'd be helping my boss out, so only good things could come from that, right? It was the worst mistake I could have made. While at work, Bruce was the most organized and process-oriented individual I had even known. His desk and files were always kept in perfect order, and never did he miss a deadline or appointment from lack of organization. However, at home he was the biggest friggin slob on the planet! You couldn't see the floor in his room as the carpet (I think there was carpet) consisted of McDonalds bags and dirty clothes. The smell was so bad that if my dog was to have an accident in the house, it most certainly would *not* be in his room.

I didn't know what to do. I was reluctant to bring it up. He was my boss! Was I supposed to tell a grown man he really needed to clean his room, as if he was my child? What if he got offended, or wanted to get back at me for embarrassing him? He could make my life miserable. Well, as you might have guessed, I did muster the courage to tell him about the way he kept his room, and things did not end well. In short, it became so nasty he finally moved out and I was transferred to another division on the ship. We were both still in the same department. However, he was no longer my direct supervisor and I have never forgotten that valuable lesson. God only knows the things he may or may not have relayed to my new supervisor and coworkers in an effort to hurt my reputation, but the lesson here is: Why take the risk?

I have known of other situations where cars and other goods were purchased, loans were made to subordinates, pet-sitting and baby-sitting arrangements exchanged, etc. I'm here to tell you from experience it's best to just steer shy of those situations. Most people are good at heart, and you shouldn't have to worry about any repercussions should things go south, but, again, when you're playing the odds, it only takes one to put your current position, or, worse, your career in jeopardy.

Attending Company Functions: I have heard many opinions on whether you should attend company functions, and most have some valid arguments. Some say you should always attend because it builds teamwork and shows your support for the company. Still others say you really should avoid these types of after-hour functions altogether, especially if alcohol is involved.

Over the years I have learned the answer really depends on the situation and the specific function, as no two functions are alike. When it comes to company functions, and whether you should attend, there are three questions you should ask yourself to help make a balanced decision.

1. *Is this truly a company-sponsored (funded) event?* There are many types of company gatherings you will experience throughout your career. From pot-luck lunches, to company-sponsored retreats that are hosted offsite, the type of event will vary. So do your research. One rule of thumb is, if it's *during working hours*, you should make damn sure you attend. Unless you have a valid, preplanned and prescheduled reason not to be there, the perceptional message you will send out will not be a good one if you are absent. I don't care if it's during your lunch and you're not getting paid, I highly advise you to show up. Remember, it's the little things that, compounded over time, can make a big difference. If it is a company-sponsored event, like a company Christmas party or awards ceremony, it's always a good idea to at least make an appearance. When confronted with a long event (2–3 hours or more) with alcohol in the mix (no pun intended), my rule of thumb is: "Don't attend, unless you will offend." Which brings me to question number two:

2. *Will you offend someone of importance (especially those who can influence your career), if you don't attend?* Even if it's not a company-funded event, if you feel you may offend

someone that has some influence on your career, then attend. But here's another rule of thumb: *just make an appearance.* I remember back in San Francisco, there was a little party being held after work to celebrate that new center's first positive sales month. It was being held at a martini bar right across the street from the center. The president of the company showed up and said, "Sorry, I can't stay long, but I just wanted to stop in and show my support and gratitude for your team's success." Ten minutes later, he was gone. That statement was brilliant! Think about it. You show up, compliment and/or congratulate the host or group, socialize for a quick ten minutes, and then respectfully leave. Simply making an appearance for 5–10 minutes can have the same positive effect as if you stayed all night long, without spending all that time and energy and forgoing any risk. And it works at any level, regardless of your position or status. Remember, even if someone else gets drunk and out of hand, or a fight breaks out, you were there. Even indirectly, you will be associated with the negative event. Guilty by association.

3. *Is there a strong career-related benefit to attending?* Notice I said *strong.* If it's a bunch of employees getting together after work for some drinks, that's not what I'd call a strong career-related benefit and we will discuss those situations later. However, if there's an event that will host a lot of influential people, those who may have an impact on your success, such as a company Christmas party, I would most surely attend. Alison Green with US News did an article back in 2012 that still holds true today. She writes:

You can raise your visibility with audiences that matter to your career. Because most company parties mix all levels of the company hierarchy in ways that don't often happen at other times of the year, you'll have a prime opportunity to network with the people who make decisions about your career. Take advantage of it by introducing yourself to company leaders who you normally don't run into. Those relationships can pay off in the future if you're trying to build support for a project or a promotion. Just make sure that you raise your visibility in the right way—by being smart and engaging, not by being the drunk guy who stumbles into them on your way back from the bathroom.

In summary, don't make a hasty decision. Take a good look at each function through *The Executive Arena* lens. Is this a function you can use to your advantage? Who will be in attendance? And if you have any doubts, you can't go wrong with the brilliant "make an appearance" approach. Lastly and most importantly, regardless of the function type you are attending or where it's being held, it's critical you never forget that *you are always working*. I'll say that again. When attending any of the aforementioned functions, remember you are always working! This is not the time and place to party. If you want to let loose and toss down a bunch of cocktails, this is *not* the time.

After-work Cocktails: As you progress through your career, I'm sure you will have plenty of opportunities to join other employees in your company for some after-work cocktails. The term "Happy Hour" was made famous by bars and clubs alike to take advantage of the corporate employee looking to wind down after a hard day at the office. However, just because this is a very popular activity in the corporate world doesn't mean you should attend as many as possible.

The best way to approach these types of situations is to use the previous "question 3" when we were analyzing company functions. *Is there a strong career-related benefit to attending?* Once again, you'll need to take a look at who's hosting it. Will other influential people be coming? Did your direct supervisor invite you? If the answer is yes, then by all means you should attend. Unfortunately, with most of these "happy hour gatherings," that's just not the case. If these sessions are regularly scheduled without fail (for example *every* Friday after work) most often they are nothing more than bitch sessions, where workers either simply gossip and spread rumors; or it's a bunch of the heavy drinkers starting their party-planned weekend a little early. I'm not saying there is anything wrong with that, I'm saying it does not "have a strong career-related benefit" and you should be cautious about getting caught up in that clique.

That said, there is a flip side to this happy-hour endeavor. Drew Hendricks, a forbes.com contributor, wrote an article in December of 2013 where he said,

> An after-work drink at a local watering hole does have its benefits. The casual atmosphere will likely lead all attendees to get to know each other better, on a more personal level, which could actually help advance careers. Those who aren't in attendance could miss a discussion that leads to a big project involving those who were there.

So you see, it's critical you take a good look at the big picture and don't forget to factor in your current level or position with the company. If you are a general employee (not yet in management) and aspire to become an executive, not attending at least some of these after-work shindigs could raise questions. Drew Hendricks goes on to say,

> Consistently saying no to outside activities can lead others to see you as not being a team player, especially if multiple others from your team are getting together. Your boss may view your refusal to participate as an indication you aren't interested in getting to know your co-workers, leading to career suicide. Avoiding social events may lead to talk around the office. Why aren't you attending? Do you have a drinking problem that has led you to avoid events involving alcohol? Is your spouse overly possessive? While you'll never be able to control the rumor mill, this personal speculation could have a detrimental effect on your career.

My wife is a senior executive in human resources and here's a perfect example. She decided to take the HR and payroll departments out for dinner to help get to know everyone and, of course, to build morale and teamwork as these events most often do. One girl, we will call Becky, decided she was too busy to attend. Now understand, Becky was already sending out some negative perceptional messages that projected to all she was unhappy at work. I even had the opportunity to meet her for all of about thirty seconds, and her negative vibrations punched me square in the face! Nevertheless, this "I can't make it" response simply solidified that she was not a good fit. Need I say Becky is no longer with the company?

Befriending subordinates: Should you become friends with those in your charge? This next topic is tricky for a couple reasons. Firstly, the line between being good "friends" and having a strong working relationship can be very blurry, to say the least. So let's address this head on. If you do things right, throughout your career you will develop some great friendships among those you work with or have worked with. One of my best friends was once my boss early in my career, and we still keep in touch to this day. Coincidentally, I actually became *his* boss later in my career, but that's a story for a later chapter. What's important here is that if you talk to any executive in today's corporate world, they will tell you "your friendship, regardless of how deep or strong, should *never* cloud your judgment when it comes to making company decisions." That's easier said than done, and we are talking about *The Executive Arena*, and *Corporate Political Intelligence*. We are all human, and when you begin to care for someone in your charge, it's only human nature to go out of your way, or in some form to do things for them you may not normally do for another employee. For example, let's say your *friend* has arrived late for work a couple times, and you need to react as their supervisor. So you privately pull them aside and say, "Look, you've been late a few times this week, and I think people are noticing. Try to make it in on time so I'm not forced to put this in writing." Take that same employee and situation and reverse the relationship. Let's say you are not friends. In fact, the offender is a poor performer that you are looking to replace. Would your reaction be different? Of course it would.

In these situations you could jeopardize your career, because others in your charge could notice your favoritism. This could bring on feelings of jealousy and weaken your team for obvious reasons. So the short answer to the question of "should you become friends with those in your charge" is almost always a resounding *no*. Almost always.

CRITICAL NOTE: For the very same reasons stated previously, if you were to ask me, "Should I befriend my *boss*, and those higher than him/her?" my answer will always be ... yes! If you have the opportunity to become friends, or otherwise personally strengthen the relationship with a supervisor, whether directly or indirectly, do it! This is how *The Executive Arena* works, and don't think for a second others are not trying to do the same. Some of the best business deals and relationships are forged over dinner or a game of golf, something outside of normal working hours.

Secondly, the exception to the rule of not befriending subordinates has to do with your position or level at the company. If you are in a management position and so is one of your subordinates—for example, you are VP and he/she is a director, I believe it's fine to become friends, even outside of work. By that time, you should be experienced enough in the world of corporate politics not to jeopardize your career, or the company, by the decisions you make through the relationships you foster. Again, do not confuse this with romantic relationships, which is never okay. However, if you are a low-level supervisor or what's called a lead employee, and you have general employees you work with, do *not* try to be their best friend. Not only is it difficult to manage properly, it can lead to problems down the road. Imagine if you were good friends and drinking buddies with those you work with and you were suddenly promoted? Now you have to go from being their friend to being their boss. It's almost impossible! You will either lose your friends, lose your job, or both. I assure you the odds of keeping both intact successfully are slim to none. This is why most of the time, when someone is promoted from within an organization, they are transferred to another department or relocated altogether. The company already knows that relationships are formed over time, and they will not take the chance of hindering company performance. In summary, analyze each situation closely and always, *always*, keep your career and its progression as the priority. Over time, as your *Corporate Political Intelligence* improves, your sixth sense (gut feeling) will tell you what you should do when confronted with these situations.

Nepotism: "I had to hire her, she's the VP's daughter!" Nepotism is another way to fish off the company pier and a way that, as an executive, you should always avoid. Some companies have a strict policy prohibiting nepotism, while others that are family owned (or started as family owned) have signs of it everywhere and at all levels. Nepotism also bleeds over to dating policies as well, again differing greatly from company to company. While both bring their own set of issues, the outcome is pretty similar. It's not good for the company or the individuals involved.

I'm sure we can all agree that hiring someone based purely on the fact that they are *family* is wrong. All hiring decisions should be based on one's qualifications and ability to do the job successfully. It should never be based on race, gender, age or any of the wonderful protected classes the government has carved into law, and rightly so. The problem with nepotism doesn't rest with whether the person is qualified. Even if you were to put aside the fact that a potential candidate was related to someone else in the company, it doesn't matter. Even if the candidate was the most qualified, and the best fit for the job, it doesn't matter. You see, it's not the candidate that's the problem, it's the *perceptions of everyone else*.

Regardless of how you justify it, or explain it to employees, they will think favoritism was involved. If the said person is promoted in the future or given an award, the fact that they are related to someone else of influence will always arise in the ranks. Feelings like this will constantly come up and can affect morale and company loyalty, and can lead to creating *Executive Arena* players like dictators, thieves, and the like, producing an atmosphere not conducive to growth and success. It's not fair to the recipient of nepotism either. Do you think it's fair to that person when people begin to say, "Be careful what you say around Bill. He's the boss's nephew." Or, "Joe only got that award because he's the president's son." In my professional opinion, nepotism is never a good idea in any organization.

Now for the small flip-side before we bring this chapter to a close. During your career, you will be exposed to situations where nepotism has entered the ranks. Perhaps it's a family-owned business, and hiring family is already a part of the company culture. In those situations, befriending those employees, or at least building a positive relationship with them, shipbuilding, as explained in the previous chapters, can be a good thing, and advantageous to your career. I'm sensing *The Executive Arena* lens is beginning to clear.

Chapter Six: - Changing Your Associations

Part One - The Five People:

"You are the average of the five people you mostly associate with." (Jim Rohn)

Jim Rohn taught many times a success principle that basically means you are the average of the five people you spend most of your time with, and it still holds true today. I would venture to change that statement just slightly to read: *You will become the average of the five people you spend most of your time with, if you're not there already.* To demonstrate this rule, let's play a little exercise. I want you to think really hard of the five people you actually spend most of your time with. Try not to include your spouse or partner, unless you absolutely have too. Who do you hang out with after work? Who is your best friend? Do you talk with someone on the phone for hours? Do you drink with a particular couple on the weekends? Who do you golf with, or fish with? Yes, you can count a couple (let's say a husband and wife for example) as one of the five, not two. Write down the name of those five people on a piece of paper and leave some space between them.

Now, for each person you put on your list, begin to jot down that person's level of success or lifestyle. In other words, ask yourself questions like: What do they do for a living? About how much do they earn per year? What kind of cars do they drive? What kind of houses do they live in? Do they own or rent? Are they happy with their current situation, or do they aspire to be more? What drives them or motivates them? You should know the answers to most of these questions, but, if not, take your best guess. Once you have all this information written down, sit back and take a look at the results. The success rule states that if you were to average out the lifestyles of your listed *five*, your personal situation is somewhere in the middle or around the same as those you associate with the most. I've done this exercise with literally hundreds of people and 95% of the time the results were right on! Of the times it was a little off, this was because the person had recently made some changes to their top five, so change was currently in motion and skewing the results. For example, if someone had just moved and made some new friends. Or perhaps another had taken up golf or was promoted and was spending considerably more time with some new acquaintances. Regardless, you can't argue with those results, and all the successful greats know, use and teach this success rule.

I adjusted Jim's original statement just slightly to read that you "will become … if you're not there already" because I want to emphasize the point that you can make a positive change at any time! Nothing is carved in stone. It's been said, if you want to be rich, watch the rich people and do what they do. Well, if you want to be a president or CEO of a company, do what they do. *Perceptional Messaging* once again comes into play here. If you want to be a successful executive, then you have to be around them. You need to begin acting like and thinking like a successful executive. The best way to start doing that is to improve your associations! Get around like-minded people and those who already have or have obtained what you want. This is another element to shipbuilding. The more time you spend with, for lack of better words, higher quality people, the quicker you will become the average of those people. Additionally, you'll begin to be *perceived* as a successful executive, by association, and the rest will follow.

Now, while this sounds simple in theory, it's not easy in practice. Depending on your own personal situation, you may have to make some tough decisions and change some of your associations, but to do that means possibly disassociating yourself from someone who may be close to you. I had a good friend I hung out with a lot. I guess you can call him my drinking buddy. We never went out and got drunk—okay, maybe a few times—but normally whenever we got together, we did have a few beers and socialize. On the surface there's nothing wrong with that, but the problem, aside from the fact that he was just scraping by financially, was he, and especially his girlfriend, were constant complainers. Negative Nellys. Whether it was the neighbors, or the weather, or the cable company, or work, or one of their clients, the list went on and on. Everything that had ever happened in their life was the fault of someone else. That kind of stuff can really wear on you, and soon *you* begin taking on the same behavior. Additionally, the neighborhood we lived in was just a stepping stone for me to a better one. However, this was where my friend was going to retire. He was settling and was content with his current lifestyle. Don't get me wrong. I'm glad he found his happiness, but his picture of paradise was very different than mine. While I really cared about him, I had to make a change, and I did.

You may have to make a similar change. I'm not saying completely remove someone from your life, unless you absolutely feel you have too, because it's very possible *you* are the change *they* are trying to make. What I mean is, perhaps they enjoy being around you because *you* are the one going places; you inspire them. Maybe you are one of their new five. Remember, the rule states it's the five you *most* associate with, so, like a diet, just cut back on the potato chips! If you normally spend five hours a week with someone, cut it back to one. If you get together every Friday night for drinks and games, cut it back to once or twice a month. You don't have to remove them from your life altogether, but don't be surprised if they seem to slip further and further away as your life begins to change and improve. It's just how it works, and that's a good thing.

So, how do you go about finding and meeting with those "new associations" we spoke of? There are many ways, and the more involved you get, the more creative you get, the easier it becomes. Let's talk about that now.

Part Two - Seek Out the Successful:

Many will say networking is a science, and a vital skill that should be learned. But calling it a science would mean it's exact. In other words, if you go to location A and do task B, you will get C. Well, that's not how it works. Networking is an art in all of its beauty and form. Where and how you go about networking depends greatly on what you are trying to accomplish. It's a skill you must turn into a habit, making it a part of your everyday routine, if you are to achieve any significant results. This is a skill every *Corporate Political Intelligence* master has in their toolbox. In other words, it should be a way of life, not a chore to perform when needed.

Those in multi-level marketing (or, should I say, the *successful* ones in multi-level marketing) understand this concept very well. They are prepared to strike up a conversation at a moment's notice and they have their business card at the ready, should they need to exchange information with someone. By the way, as a side note don't knock multi-level marketing companies like Amway, LegalShield, Pampered Chef, Nerium, Mary Kay and the like. I know many people, including myself, that have made a decent living with multi-level marketing companies. Some people, who I know personally, went on to be multi-millionaires. I bring this up because, regardless of their product or service, or what you may personally feel about how they operate, their training and support models are second to none. What all these companies promote and teach are some of the best and most proven business and personal success techniques in the world. They live by the teachings of such greats as Jim Rohn, Jack Canfield, Jeff Olsen, Tony Robbins, Zig Zigler, Bob Proctor, Wayne Dyer, Ken Blanchard, Joe Vitale and many more. You too should seek out the knowledge of these great teachers, and we will discuss that in a later chapter. You can find a list of my personal favorites in the resources section of this book or by going to www.ArenaTrilogy.com.

Additionally, don't be afraid to talk to strangers. The easiest way to strike up a conversation is to ask someone about themselves. Humans love to talk about themselves and their achievements, so ask questions about their life and successes. Your questions should not be intrusive, but inviting. To get the conversation started, ask questions like: This is my first time here, do you like this place? So, what do you do for a living? Are you a native of Florida (or whatever state/city you are in)? Where did you grow up? Once you get the ball rolling it should be pretty easy to maintain a conversation. Just remember, this is not an act. Your goal is to *genuinely* get to know someone, and hopefully make a new friend or association. You will be pleasantly surprised when you realize that the other person is trying to do the same thing. It's what successful people do!

Upgrade where you hang out:

So how do you *seek out the successful?* The first step is to go where they go. If you are going to change your associations and "up your game," then I don't know any other way of saying it: *you need to elevate the class of people you are around.* Let's face it, if your favorite watering hole sells $1.50 draft beers, and the restroom smells like a port-a-potty (or *is* port-a-potty), that's a pretty good indication it's not a place to meet the extremely successful, with the exception of the owner of the establishment. You need to change it up. A good rule of thumb to remember is: "The successful play where others won't pay." In other words, the person who lives for the Friday night $1.50 draft specials doesn't hang out where that same draft beer is $7.50 or more. The same is true when it comes to dining. There's nothing wrong with these cheap eating establishments and local watering holes. I have had my share of these great little local places, and they are awesome for what they are. But my reason for patronizing these places was not to meet other successful people.

It all comes down to understanding this: *Where* one should seek out the successful is all relative, so you need to *upgrade* the way you think as well. I remember when I was young my mom would say things like: "We are going out for a fancy dinner at Red Lobster." Now think about that statement for a minute. Perhaps you wouldn't consider Red Lobster or Olive Garden a fancy dinner (or maybe you would); but for, let's say, a family of five who lives on a combined household income of around $35,000 a year, Red Lobster is an absolute treat and could be considered a "fancy dinner." Now take the senior executive whose annual income is just over $200,000. What would they consider a "fancy dinner"? I assure you it's *not* Red Lobster. First of all, I doubt they would use the term "fancy dinner" and, instead, would describe it as either a "nice" or "quiet dinner." Secondly, for most of us at that level, dropping $150–$200 on dinner isn't a special event at all. In fact, it's just dinner. See where I'm coming from here? It's all relative, and it's your job to start thinking *as if* you were already successful. Where would you go for a cocktail? Where would you go for some fun or for lunch? I'll let you in on a little secret. Believe it or not, you will find more successful people *during lunch* than you will dinner at what I call level-1 places, such as Red Lobster, Olive Garden, Applebee's, etc. Taking it up a notch, good level-2 places to perhaps have a glass of wine, lunch and even dinner are PF Changs, Cheesecake Factory, Carrabba's, Bonefish Grill and other establishments at that level. Remember, most of these level-2 places also have bars inside, so you can have lunch, mingle and meet some very interesting and successful people, and not be stuck in a booth making it difficult (or even weird) to attempt to strike up a conversation. Believe it or not, a lot of business meetings and business-related meet-ups happen at level-2 places, even for dinner.

The beach (if you are lucky to live near the ocean) is another place to meet other successful people. Of course, there is always a mixture of class at the beach, but it's not hard to notice who's just a tourist and who's a local, who's successful and who's not. Again, the area and type of establishments that accompany the beachfront will give you a good indication of the type of people that frequent that area. Other establishments that are actually on the water are great as well. They don't have to be the "beach" *per se*, with sand and umbrellas. There are many boating and yacht clubs as well as other establishments with great water views you could frequent. It's not rocket science. The costlier the establishment or area, the more affluent the customer or resident. It's that simple.

I'm guessing by now you are thinking you will have to spend a little more money if you want to meet and hang with the more successful people. Well, you would be right. You will need to break out of your old habits, stop looking for the best deals on food, drink, entertainment, and go find new people with whom to associate. Remember, this is an investment in yourself, and you are on a mission to change your associations. You want to soar with the eagles, not hang with the pigeons. I'm not saying be stupid and blow money foolishly. Get creative! For example, if your budget for an evening of eats and drinks is $50, then it's better to go to a higher-end place for just two hours and make some great new associations than it is to go to a place where the same $50 could last all night. I'll take two glasses of fine wine for a total cost of $30 while networking with some very successful people, over that same $30 in cheap beer, getting toasty all night with those who will do nothing for my success. Get the picture? It's a change of mindset, so get out there and be creative. You know the area you live in better than I do. Use that knowledge, bring your spouse or partner, and go meet some great people. This element of shipbuilding is an art that will pay huge dividends in the future. Aside from upgrading your associations, you may just meet your future employer or business partner, so get out there and do it!

Golf:

Finally, there is the _ultimate_ meeting place, sport, business venue, eating establishment, and watering hole on the planet when it comes to changing your associations. If you want to meet other successful people, there is no other activity that brings together the best elements of business and pleasure, breeding success and quality associations. You guessed it: _golf!_

If you don't golf, I highly recommend you learn and learn quickly. You don't have to be great, just learn the basics and have fun. In fact, most golfers that you see on a golf course are not very good at all. Only about 5–10%, depending on the course, are even decent players, while the other 95% or so are actually horrible from a professional standpoint. And here's the kicker: no one cares! Believe it or not, 80% of golfers will _never_ get below an eighteen handicap. When I first started golfing—I'm talking my first year on the links—I was hitting anywhere from a 100 to 115. I was horrible, but I was also having a great time and meeting some great people. A year later I was in the low nineties, and only once have I ever broken into the eighties.

Ben Simms was a pro golfer who taught me how to golf by coaching me through eighteen holes some years ago. It was a team-building event put on by a college I was working for long ago. He told me, "You should shoot for bogie golf." That's one over par on *every hole*! That's eighteen over when it's all said and done. I learned if you can achieve bogie golf, you are in good company with the majority of golfers you will meet.

My whole point is, don't worry about how good or bad you may be at golf, because it doesn't matter. The goal with golf is twofold. Firstly, you can't help but meet other professionals, as most courses will send you out in groups of four. Secondly, a lot of business talk and business deals occur on the golf course. It's generally quiet, relaxing, and you get some one-on-one time with whoever is in the cart with you. Thirdly, I shouldn't have to say this but this applies to women as well. Golf is no longer a "man's sport," and those who still believe it is are just assholes. Sorry, just keeping it real.

Jenn Harris, CEO of High Heel Golfer, Inc. wrote an article for PGA.com in 2014 titled "6 Reasons Golf is Good for Business." In this article she writes that golf:

1. *Provides access to an environment where business deals are done.*
2. *Challenges women to go beyond their comfort zone.*
3. *Instills confidence both on and off the course.*
4. *Gives insight into how to read others.*
5. *Offers you a sneak peek into the integrity and ethics of your golf partners.*

Let's you open up and have fun.

Please take note that points four and five have everything to do with increasing your *Corporate Political Intelligence*. Even more amazingly, she goes on to explain some enlightening statistics. If you still don't buy into the whole "golf is good for your career," chew on these for a bit: "Executives who play golf make 17% more than those who don't. 54% of business professionals see golf as the perfect networking tool." And the one that really hits home: "An estimated 90% of all Fortune 500 CEOs play golf." She writes much more on this topic, but you get the picture. The benefits of playing golf greatly outweigh the fear of not being a great player, so throw away the excuses and hit the links! Consider golf an investment in your career.

Golf can be a bit pricey, with an average round of golf around $35–$40 plus your cart fee (fee to rent a golf cart). Some courses are more, some less. It all depends on the actual course. But again, remember the previous lesson on the *cost of a particular establishment*, and the type of people that frequent there? So, get some clubs, learn how to golf, get in there and meet some successful people.

I suggest you begin with a starter set of clubs, a pair of golf shoes, some balls and a glove. I bought my first starter set of brand new clubs for a couple hundred bucks. You may be able to get a nice set of used clubs for even less. Don't go nuts trying to purchase expensive high-end clubs until you learn more about the game, your swing and how you personally golf. If you're new to golf, it's better to buy a cheap set of clubs and purchase a few hours of professional lessons. Also, never lie about your golf experience. It's okay and a very accepted practice to tell everyone you're new to the game, and that you just purchased that set of clubs. Believe it or not, a lot of fellow golfers will be more than happy to show you the ropes and give you some tips to improve your game. Sometimes too many!

Lastly, there are the few—very few—highly competitive golfers that can't go out for an afternoon of golf without having some form of money on the line. Worse yet, they are the loud ones you will hear at the clubhouse bitching about their game, another player, the course, the care or upkeep of the course or the greens, etc. They get frustrated by their score, get upset with other players and frankly prevent others from having a good time. They are what is called the *Ego Golfer*, more interested in feeding their ego than enjoying the game and the people who play it. But they are not the majority. Simply steer clear of this type of golfer and focus on enjoying the game, enjoying the people you are with, and building business and personal relationships that will last a lifetime. I assure you, it's worth every penny you invest.

Volunteer:

As we pulled up next to the cage, Shadow began to quickly pace back and forth as if she knew it was her turn to be fed. For Shadow, nothing was more important at that moment than to eat, so my job was to stay focused, show respect, not fear, do my job and feed her. I grabbed the white plastic five-gallon bucket, already filled with a pre-measured amount of raw beef, pork and chicken parts, off the back of the keeper's golf cart and headed over to her cage. As I approached, Shadow stopped pacing and positioned her nose right by the opening between the fence post and gate. She growled and stared at me. There was about a three- to four-inch gap where we could easily slip through large pieces of meat and poultry for her to grab, but not big enough for her head to get through and bite *your* head off. However, you had to be extremely careful because you could still get your hand bitten or bitten off if your hands went past those steel fence posts. As I grabbed a large raw chicken quarter from the bucket, Shadow snarled and stared intently. Holding the chicken quarter by the leg bone, I quickly slipped the thigh portion through the steel bars and Shadow immediately sank her two-inch pearly whites into it, aggressively yanking it from my hand. She turned slightly away from my position as her powerful jaws crushed the chicken bones as if they were saltine crackers and devoured the first piece in about ten seconds. She had finally eaten her first piece, and now would be much calmer for the remainder of her breakfast.

If you haven't guessed by now, Shadow was a tiger. A big beautiful white tiger that had luckily found her forever home at a wonderful place called Elmira's Wildlife Sanctuary in Wimauma, Florida. Elmira's Wildlife Sanctuary rescues and provides forever homes for wild/exotic animals. From tigers and bears to lemurs and parrots, Elmira's Wildlife Sanctuary is one of the most amazing non-profit organizations that operates and depends 100% on the efforts of its volunteers and the private donations from those who believe in their cause.

When I first moved to the Tampa Bay area, someone on our community Facebook page posted that Elmira's Wildlife Sanctuary was looking for some volunteer animal keepers! "Animal keepers?" I asked myself out loud. My wife and I love animals and have rescued our share of dogs in our lifetime (we currently have seven), so I jumped on the opportunity. It was very, very hard work, especially during the hot and wet summer months here in south Florida. However, it was also the most gratifying eighteen months of my life. I met some wonderful people, made some great friends and connections, while at the same time giving back to my community, giving time to a wonderful cause, and helping save the lives of and befriend some of nature's most beautiful creatures. In return I was filled with a great sense of satisfaction, love and gratitude, which led to attracting more great things into my life that I could be grateful for. You've heard the phrase "Karma is a bitch," right? Well, you need to understand that Karma, the Universe, the Law of Attraction, or whatever you want to call it, works on the positive side of the spectrum as well. Do good things for others, and the universe will, in turn, provide people, circumstances and events that will bring more good things into your life.

We will discuss the Law of Attraction and how to use it in a later book called *The Abundance Arena*, but for now just know that volunteering is by far one of the most effective ways to meet other very passionate, like-minded people. Let's chat about some other great places you can volunteer in your own community .

The Humane Society, or your local "dog pound" as it once was called, is always looking for volunteers. Your local soup kitchen or homeless shelters are other great ways to give back and meet some wonderful people. I know many very senior executives that do great work with the homeless and in similar programs. Not all volunteer opportunities are with non-profit organizations. Most schools are looking for parents to help out from time to time with special events, the PTSO (Parents, Teachers, Students Organization), even becoming classroom moms (and dads), and it's growing!

Veterinary clinics are great places to volunteer your time, as is getting involved with community sports programs and other organizations like the Cub Scouts, the Sea Cadets, Civil Air Patrol, Girl Scouts, etc. The point here is that volunteering can help your career in many ways. It helps you network and meet other passionate people. It provides you with a sense of satisfaction that you are giving back, and it makes you feel energized and appreciated. Finally, let's not forget the perceptional message you are sending out to all those who know you spend some of your free time volunteering. There is simply no downside.

Points to Remember:

1. You will become the average of the five people you mostly associate with. If you want to improve your quality of life, you must improve the quality of your associations.

2. If you want to become a success, study what the successful do, and *do* what they do. For example, if you want to make $100,000 a year, don't take advice on how to make that amount of money from those who have never made that much themselves. Believe me, everyone wants to give you their opinion. While they may mean well, it will not serve you.

3. Upgrade the type of establishments you frequent. To seek out the successful, you need to hang where the successful hang. Join their groups and, again, do what they do. Go for the single $15 glass of wine establishment over the ten $1.50 draft beer holes in the wall. Golf, volunteer, give back!

4. Let go of those who are living the lifestyle you don't want. Stop associating with, or at least limit your contact with, those who currently live the level of lifestyle you are trying to escape or improve. Make the change, and change will come.

Chapter Seven: Selecting and Using a Confidant

Aside from the excruciating heat during the summer, I absolutely loved Las Vegas. Not for the gambling, legal prostitution, or the biggest collection of strip clubs on the planet, though for some that's a plus, but more so for the *energy* that permeates the air while you are there. They say New York is the city that never sleeps, but I've been to both places and Las Vegas takes the cake in that respect. There are great shows, cheap flights and the dining is to die for, which I'm sure is why so many companies choose Las Vegas as their annual conference location. My company at the time was no different. With thirty-one locations around the country, Las Vegas was the best place financially to hold our annual GMs conference. Flights were cheap, as was the food, and we could easily find a hotel that would house all of us at a very nice group rate. More importantly, the night life would provide everyone a good time, with good variety and a chance to get to know each other.

> **Executive Arena Rule**: During an annual conference or large offsite company function, your time spent with colleagues *after hours* can prove just as valuable to building relationships and your career *if not more* than the time spent in official meetings and break-out sessions.

My wakeup call at the Embassy Suites was right on time at 6:00 a.m. I quickly showered, dressed for the day and headed down to partake in their omelets-to-order breakfast. Our meetings didn't begin until 9:00 a.m., but I hated rushing, so I always got an early start on the day. When I got downstairs, I headed to the wide-open lobby, crossed over a small bridge that stretched across a beautiful indoor koi pond, a trademark of Embassy Suites, to get in line to place my order. To my surprise Kevin, the president of the company, was getting in line as well. I had been waiting for an opportunity like this for a while, so now seemed as good a time as any. As we waited for our omelets, I said, "Hey, Kevin, can I ask you for a favor?"

"Absolutely," he replied with a smile, "… within reason." He winked to indicate this was going to be a light conversation.

"Well, I've always been a believer that you can never stop learning, and there is always room for improvement."

"I agree with that," he tossed in quickly.

"Well, while I know we *all* have annual reviews, I was wondering if maybe once a month or so, informally of course, we could meet for a few minutes to basically just go over how I'm doing professionally, and perhaps even discuss any areas, if any, I can improve on as well? I'm just looking to be better."

There was a short pause as Kevin held out his plate to accept the omelet he had ordered from the chef. I wasn't sure if he'd agree to anything like this, but it was worth a shot. I did report directly to him, so I wasn't going over anyone's head, but still, the request was a little out of the ordinary. There were two other VPs like myself that reported directly to Kevin, none of whom had a monthly informal meeting with him.

After a short pause that felt like eternity ... "Could we do this over the phone if our schedules don't line up for a face to face?" Kevin asked.

"Absolutely," I replied. "Like I said, just an informal discussion, and I could also use this time to get advice from you on certain challenges I may be facing in the field."

"Sounds like a plan," Kevin confirmed. "Send me a meeting invite each month—because I'll never remember—and we'll go from there."

Music to my ears.

This was the start of a great relationship and the initial forming of a future *confidant*. It's important to understand here that I didn't do this just to "get one over" on the other VPs. Of course, that's a positive byproduct of the situation, but I did it to truly improve myself. For one, having some one-on-one time with the president of the company on a regular basis is a huge plus. But, more importantly, having a mentor or confidant that also has influence on your career is invaluable. I didn't do anything malicious towards my fellow colleagues, like bad mouth them. I kept my integrity.

Kevin as well as some select others, including Bob from a few pages ago, became great coaches, mentors and confidants throughout my career. It's vital you constantly seek out and foster relationships that could lead to mentor-type relationships. Don't be surprised if these types of relationships lead to personal friendship as well. That can be a bonus too as long as it remains platonic. Any deeper relationship beyond friends can and most times will *prove disastrous.*

So, just what is a confidant? A confidant can take many forms, be it an executive coach that one pays for, or a best friend you run ideas past from time to time. There are many definitions depending on the source, so, for the sake of argument, let's look at the definition from dictionary.com. It defines a confidant (confidante) as: "a close friend or associate to whom secrets are confided or with whom private matters and problems are discussed." Not a bad definition. This is basic, but a good confidant goes much deeper in context. Here is *The Executive Arena* definition: *A confidant is a person who is or was a colleague, from whom you can seek advice with certain problems, or solutions to problems, in complete confidence, without the fear of judgment or reprisal.* As the word confidant denotes, it's someone you can confide in, and who in turn can give you sound advice. Some call their confidant a mentor, or personal coach, but whatever name you give that person, don't confuse a confidant/mentor with a certified or executive coach. An executive coach is someone you pay in return for a service. They are normally from outside your industry, and their goal is to help you achieve your full potential, through thought-provoking conversations and processes. They have no attachment or commitment to business outcomes, as their main focus is motivating and coaching you as a person. Some call executive coaches "business shrinks," as some conversations can touch on childhood experiences, past failures and other performance blockers that can have an effect on how you handle certain situations. An executive coach can be a valuable asset in relation to your long-term goals, but that is a topic for another book.

The ultimate goal with any confidant is the *transfer of knowledge* from them to you. As mentioned in a previous chapter, you want to be perceived as an expert in your field, so knowledge transfer is a priority. While some confidants may have more business experience than you, that's not always the case. While "more" can be good, "different" can be even better. Sometimes you just need a fresh set of eyes (or ears) to consider a situation from a different perspective. Bob, who we talked about previously, was one of those confidants. You see, while he was *my* boss early in my career, we developed a strong business relationship that eventually blossomed into friendship. We became each other's confidants and would regularly meet to discuss problems, challenges and other business-related topics, sometimes even over a beer or two. Then later in our careers, long after we had both moved on to other opportunities, I actually hired Bob to work for me! Now I was his boss, and the close mentorship began once again, just in reverse. You may be wondering if that was a difficult arrangement. How can someone go from boss to subordinate and vice versa, in addition to being good personal friends? Was there any tension, animosity, jealousy, resentment? The answer is *no* and for two reasons. First, both Bob and I understood the value of having a confidant. We didn't regard each other as threats and think, "He has more experience than I do" or "He got lucky landing this job or that job." We understood that our individual skills, talents and experiences were just different, not superior. We also understood we were life-long learners in *The Executive Arena* and can learn something new every day, regardless of where the lesson comes from. The *source* of knowledge is irrelevant; it's what you do with it that determines its value.

Selection: So how does one go about finding and developing a confidant? What type of person would be most beneficial towards achieving your goals and aspirations? While the answer to these questions can vary depending on your personal needs, here are some important guidelines to help you find and cultivate that perfect mentor relationship!

1. Ideally, a confidant should be someone in your organization, or at the very least in your particular industry. They should be someone who has walked in your shoes ("been there done that") and can teach you about the sometimes unwritten rules and culture of the company/industry.

2. They should be someone you admire personally and professionally, not just someone who is at a higher level or position than you. In other words, they should be someone who is an inspiration to you. Ask yourself these questions:

    a. Do I want to achieve what that person has achieved?
    b. Would I be happy, and/or do I aspire to someday hold that person's position or achieve that same level (e.g., director, vice president, etc.)?
    c. Because of this person's past experiences and positions, would I value the advice from them?

3. Your confidant should be well respected and have credibility within your particular organization or industry.

If your confidant is considered abrasive, standoffish, or just not respected within the organization, regardless of their current job performance, they will not make a good confidant, nor will your association with that person deliver a positive perceptional message. They must have credibility in the organization, so don't let your choice of confidant be tainted by a person's title alone. For example, throughout my career I've known many at the director level that have earned more credibility in the company than those with a VP or senior VP title. A title is just that, a title. While it can denote a specific level of achievement, sometimes it does not. I knew an outdoor sales company that gave the title "vice president of sales" to all their sales people. Another called their sales reps "area sales managers" in an attempt to give them some sort of credibility in the eyes of the consumer. So do not rely on title alone; look at the substance.

4. Lastly, and perhaps the most important element in a successful confidant, is *trust*. Can you trust your confidant, and can he/she trust you? In short, can you both keep a secret? Throughout your career, you will be exposed to and perhaps might even need to share sensitive information. It's vital to be able to discuss sensitive topics and situations with your confidant without the fear of information leaks. Imagine if you were considering the pros and cons of replacing a specific employee, and you discussed the options with your confidant, only to find out your intentions were now spreading throughout your department. You were not sure it was a good idea, so you wanted another opinion. But now, rumors have begun to fly about how you are going to fire someone and now everyone is on edge. Not

a good picture. Make sure you can trust each other, and don't be afraid to bring up the topic of trust with your confidant directly. It will set the stage for a long-term beneficial relationship.

Approach: Okay, so let's assume you now have a few ideas about who would make a good confidant, but you're wondering just how to approach someone about that. You may be asking yourself: How well do you have to know the person before making an attempt at a closer professional relationship? First let me say, you don't have to be best friends when considering someone for confidant status. The whole point of a confidant is the *transfer of knowledge*. The strong relationship, in most cases, will come later. As for how you make the initial approach, here are a few ideas that have worked in the past for myself and others.

1. *Just ask*: Can you just walk up and say, "Hey, will you be my confidant?" Well, actually, yes that's one way, but I don't think you should use those exact words. Take the previous example I gave you at the beginning of the chapter. I didn't come right out and ask Kevin to be my confidant. However, I did set the stage for him to be just that. I asked him for regularly scheduled informal meetings to discuss issues, challenges, etc., and it was my hope that, over time, it would grow into a confidant-type relationship, which it did. In other words, don't ask for cake, just ask for the ingredients.
2. *Seek advice*: If the person you are considering isn't someone you normally collaborate with, then bring to them a specific problem or challenge, and ask for advice. Swing by their office (or pick up the phone) and ask if

they have a few minutes, because you would like their input on a situation or problem. Just make sure the problem is genuine. People naturally want to help, so it's a great way to begin a relationship. By seeking advice you are also sending the perceptional message to that person that you respect and value their opinion. What better way to begin an information exchange? Additionally, you are killing two birds with one stone, because you are also solving a problem or situation while befriending a colleague. Just remember, *before you leave, set the stage for future meetings.* Thank them for their time, tell them you value their input and ask if it's okay to "run things by them" from time to time. If you do it right, I'm sure the response will be positive.

3. *It just happens:* Sometimes the confidant relationship just happens naturally. My wife, who's a senior executive in human resources, had hired a business consultant to come in to one of her previous companies to help mentor and coach the senior management team. Let's call him Randy. He worked very closely with Sharon and, over time, they were extremely impressed with each other's talents and abilities. A strong business relationship formed, and the project was a huge success. Since then, Sharon has moved on to bigger and better things. However, they still communicate to this day, sometimes on a weekly basis, if for nothing more than to recap the week's events. I know I said it's best if your confidant comes from within your company or industry. However in this case, though Randy was an outside consultant, he came from a human resources background and has his PhD in organizational psychology, which is the perfect

confidant for an executive in the human resources industry.

Usage: When to call upon your confidant and for what reason is entirely up to you and is based on the type and strength of your relationship. For example, I can grab my cell at 10:00 p.m. on a Saturday night and call Bob to get his opinion on a situation if I choose. For others, during normal working hours may be best. Which brings me to another important point: you can have more than one confidant and most likely will as you progress through your career. Napoleon Hill, in his best-selling book *Think and Grow Rich*, talks about having a mastermind group. It's basically the old adage "two heads are better than one." Your inner circle of contacts will grow and change over time. Different people will possess different skills and talents on which you can call depending on the situation. It's all about shipbuilding, adding tools to your *Executive Arena* tool box, and being perceived as an expert in your field. In the past I've used my confidants to discuss many things, both personal and professional, including, but not limited to:

- Problem employees: do I continue to train and coach, or cut my losses?

- How do I get noticed on my next project?

- To get another opinion on the TV commercial I produced before it goes live.

- When recruiting for a critical position, what best traits should I be looking for?

- Taking the next step in my career, like switching jobs or industries.

- When building or inheriting a new team or department.

- Personnel conflicts or clashes and how to resolve them.

There are many beneficial reasons for using a confidant. From everyday management tasks to career guidance, a confidant, mentor, even an executive coach, can play an important role in your success.

So, in short, call upon your confidant or mastermind group as much as needed, being cautious not to look as though you need help with every decision, especially if your confidant is within the company, or happens to be your direct supervisor. Whenever I have to make a serious or critical decision, even though I may be 90% sure of the direction I'm going, I reach out. It doesn't hurt. Sometimes it's just good to get a new set of eyes to take a look, if nothing more than to solidify your decision or train of thought. Being confident in your decisions regardless of the outcome is a good thing. Of course, if you end up being right, that's always a plus.

Points to Remember:

1. During an annual conference or large offsite company function, your time spent with colleagues after hours can prove just as valuable in building relationships and your career as the time spent in official meetings. Remember, I said time with colleagues, not with others. Don't use a conference as an excuse to party.

2. Having a confidant that also has influence on your career is invaluable. A boss or someone with credibility from inside your company is optimal.

3. The ultimate goal with having any confidant is the *transfer of knowledge* from them to you. Remember, you want to be perceived as an expert in your field, so knowledge transfer is critical. Having a wealth of knowledge you can pull from at a moment's notice is extremely beneficial. No one cares *how* you get the right answer; what's important is you *have* the right answer!

4. The most important element in a successful mentorship is *trust*. In short, can you both keep a secret? It's vital to be able to discuss sensitive topics and situations with your confidant without the fear of information leaks.

5. You can have more than one confidant and most likely will as you progress through your career. It's called having a mastermind group. It's basically the old adage "two heads are better than one." Your inner circle of contacts should grow and change over time, and that's a good thing, because it means *you* are growing and changing in your career.

Chapter Eight: Behind Closed Doors - The Sometimes "Necessary" Dark Side

"If you know the enemy and know yourself, you need not fear the result of a hundred battles. If you know yourself but not the enemy, for every victory gained you will also suffer a defeat. If you know neither the enemy nor yourself, you will succumb in every battle." (Sun Tzu, *The Art of War*)

So far we have discussed *The Executive Arena* in a *positive* light. Thus we have focused on employing *Corporate Political Intelligence* in a favorable way. However, I would be remiss if we did not discuss the dark and sometimes necessary tactics that you may and most likely will see employed at some point throughout your career. I'm not speaking about the guy who's talking behind your back as the stomper would, or the one who's stealing your ideas, like the thief discussed previously. In this chapter we will focus on the more covert tactics that are employed at a much higher level. I'm talking about situations where usually two or more management team members get together, behind closed doors, to devise a stratagem for the betterment or protection of a team, department, division or even the company as a whole. When deciding whether to employ these stratagems, the issue is most often "What's best for the company?" or "Everyone will be much happier." Unfortunately, while that may be true in some cases, a good portion of these *dark tactics* are born and fueled in large part by poor or nonexistent company processes or policies. In other words, people find ways around rules and regulations to achieve their goals, finding loopholes in the company's armor. Regardless of how or when these tactics are put into play, it's crucial to recognize when these tactics are used, and what to do when, God forbid, *you* are the target, whether directly or indirectly.

The Peter Principle: Tara was a decent instructor. She joined our training company just a few months ago and, based on the student evaluations that were collected after each eight-hour class, her overall grade was satisfactory, to just above satisfactory. In short about a seven to eight on a ten-point scale. She wasn't the best, but she did her job. I guess you could call her a Steady Eddie. However, the unwritten rule at this company was that anything less than a nine or ten on a student evaluation was considered below average, so receiving even straight eights from all your students was *not* a good evaluation. But Tara's student evaluations were not her biggest problem. While she did what was expected of her in class, outside of the classroom Tara was very vocal, even sometimes abrasive towards her colleagues. For some reason Tara found it necessary to loudly share the fact that she had sued her last two employers for wrongful termination. She spoke of it so often it was as though she was actually proud of her past work history. She had claimed she was fired for being a woman at one company, and then fired again at her next place of employment for being a minority. She was so vocal that management soon became aware and concerned about her behavior. A red flag had now been raised.

As time went on, her colleagues began to avoid her altogether when possible, which, of course, made things worse. The proverbial *chip on her shoulder* was the perceptional message being received by her coworkers. Tara's boisterous behavior grew and became very disruptive, which had a significant effect on the training team's morale. It was time for management to get involved.

None of what Tara was claiming ever came out during her interview process. In fact, her previous employer was never contacted because she had stated on her application that she was "currently employed" with said employer. However, now that Tara was no longer working for that company, management decided to reach out to the company for a reference check to see if she had lied on her application. All the company could tell us was Tara was "*not* eligible for rehire." The second red flag was now raised. Tara was confronted directly by management, and I had the privilege of being present at that meeting, along with John, the general manager, and Susan, the human resources manager. We all thought it best to have HR present just to make sure nothing got out of hand, as well as to have a neutral witness. I'll skip the pleasantries and get right to the meat of the conversation.

"Tara, I know we covered this in your initial interview a few months ago," John began, "but would you remind us once again why you decided to leave your last place of employment?"

Tara seemed a bit taken back by the question but quickly replied, "For better promotional opportunities. I wasn't going anywhere at the last company."

John nodded as he opened Tara's personnel file, picked up a specific page, which I assumed was her interview notes or application, and asked, "Well it says here you were currently employed at the time of your interview, which would indicate you resigned after you got our offer of employment."

"That's right," Tara injected quickly and confidently.

John continued, "However, from what I hear, you've been telling people you were fired from your last job for being a minority … and you sued them. I'm just trying to get to the truth."

We could all see the anger building up in Tara's face. "I'm not sure where you are getting your information from," Tara replied very defensively, "but I did leave the company. I was not fired! They didn't treat me fairly so I started looking for another job. And so what if I did sue them? That's no one's business but my own."

"You're exactly right," John agreed, "it is your own business. So I suggest you keep your business to yourself, and stop spreading *your business* around the office. Do I make myself clear?"

The meeting concluded.

We never brought up the fact that we already knew she was fired from her last job. There was no reason to. However, there was also a lot we did not know. Did Tara really sue her last two employers? Were her last two employers really scumbags, and did both unjustly terminate her? Was it because of performance or something else? Regardless of the answers to those questions, management agreed Tara had to go. All the turmoil she had already caused among her peers, and the fact that she had not been honest with management since day one, solidified the decision of termination. However, the last thing the company wanted was to be sued for wrongful termination, especially when it wasn't true. Management unanimously agreed if they simply terminated Tara for cause, she would most certainly file a complaint at least. If the company was sued, or a claim was filed with unemployment, they wanted to be sure their chances of winning were high. So, what were they to do? How could they ensure Tara would not win an unjust wrongful termination complaint or lawsuit? Simple ... Tara was promoted.

The *Peter Principle* is a theory originated by Dr. Laurence J. Peter and basically states: "In a hierarchy, successful employees tend to rise to their level of incompetence." In other words, one will tend to get promoted and keep getting promoted to the specific level where they no longer have the skills/aptitude to do the job successfully. Again, this was Jerry's problem, mentioned in a previous chapter. His *Corporate Political Intelligence* was so high, he would get promoted very quickly, most times to a level he was not ready for. This is why his "successes" were short lived. Not to beat a dead horse, but this is why being good at your job, and always striving for improvement, is so important in *The Executive Arena.*

Tara's situation was a little different. Firstly, as you might have already realized, Tara had no *Corporate Political Intelligence* whatsoever. So the Peter Principle was used as a weapon against her. To bring this story to its climactic ending, Tara was promoted to training manager. Her job was now to manage the teaching schedules of over fifty-five instructors, audit classes, assist in the new hire process, while at the same time keeping up her own teaching schedule. It was a position management knew she would fail at. Within thirty days, Tara had received numerous verbal warnings about her performance, and was written up twice for not achieving specific weekly benchmarks. She was terminated for performance on day forty-five into her new role, after receiving a final warning, and, as expected, she filed for unemployment stating it was a *wrongful termination* due to racial bias. During arbitration, the company not only provided all the documentation to prove she was underperforming in her management role; more importantly, they were able to counter her claim of racial bias by showing proof she was "recently *promoted* because she was a good instructor." Tara's claim was dismissed. She did not receive unemployment benefits, and we never heard from her again. It's also important to note here that human resources was not part of the decision to use the Peter Principle as a weapon against Tara. All HR knew was that she was promoted and was now failing at her job. "That's all HR needed to know" was management's mentality in this situation. When it came time to terminate her, HR simply made sure management had all the proper documentation to do so, which of course they did.

Whether you perceive this situation and ultimate outcome as right, wrong or indifferent is irrelevant. The point here is to show you the dark side of corporate politics and the lengths that some, whether an individual or a represented organization, will go to achieve a specific outcome when threatened.

Being set-up for failure: If someone wants to get rid of a "problem" employee, regardless of their performance, there is always a way. That said, the difficulty level in performing such a covert task is based on the current company's three "Ps": processes, policies and procedures. For example, most processes, policies and procedures regarding a sales department are put in place to ensure fairness, promote a friendly yet competitive environment, while preventing favoritism. Sales goals, the metrics involved in monitoring those goals, as well as the training received, tools provided, and lead distribution guidelines should all be written in stone. They should be clearly understood by all team members and strictly enforced by management. Unfortunately, in many situations that's not the case, and it opens the door to foul play, even by management personnel themselves. Here are some examples:

1. *Lead Distribution:* This is one of the most common tactics used to get rid a problem employee, especially in sales. Too often there are no guidelines regarding the amount, type and frequency at which a person should receive sales leads. More often than not, who gets a certain lead is arbitrarily based on the opinion or needs of the sales manager or organization. In addition, if you've ever been in sales, you know there are weak leads, average leads and some very strong leads. They all have to do with *closing percentage*, or having the best chance at making a sale (for those non-sales people types). These classifications are known in the industry as cold, warm, and hot leads. The

sales manager, or whoever is doing lead distribution, knows the difference in the *quality* of a lead coming in, and can easily forward the best leads to the person or persons of their choice. This in itself makes it very easy for someone to "blackball" another employee, because it's not based on the *number* of leads one receives, which is easily measurable and documented. Instead it's based on the *quality* of the lead, which is much harder to trace or prove when one is being wronged. That said, the favoritism that sometimes occurs is not always malicious. In most sales environments, the sales manager or sales management as a whole is under a lot of pressure to achieve specific sales goals month after month. Because of this consistent pressure, especially when in a pinch, management will tend to give the best leads to his/her best sales people. It's typical to do this, and I've witnessed this firsthand many times. To the novice observer this seems like the right thing to do, but it's not. While it will bring short-term fiscal successes, these types of practices can hinder sales team growth, give rise to unhealthy competition and increase turnover. How to properly lead a sales team will be covered in a later book called *The Leadership Arena*, but for now it's crucial you recognize these behaviors, then decide whether the behavior you are observing is the result of malicious intent or sales pressure induced.

2. *Being Shunned:* Another way to rid the company of an unwanted employee is called "Being Shunned." The objective here is to employ specific tactics to the point where the target (employee) just leaves the company on their own. This is most beneficial for the company because there is less paperwork, no unemployment

benefits need to be paid, department and/or company morale is not adversely affected, and the chances of a lawsuit is significantly reduced because the employee resigned. This is sometimes accomplished by making the employee feel unneeded, or, worse yet, unwanted. Sometimes, in the most desperate circumstances, it's a combination of both. Here are some of those tactics explained in detail:

a. <u>Micromanagement:</u> Yes, there are bosses that micromanage as part of their management style. However if, all of a sudden, micromanagement comes into play, where there once wasn't any, you should take notice. Dominique Rodgers, a *Monster* contributor, wrote an article called, "How to Tell if Your Company is Hoping You'll Quit." In this article he writes:

You're used to being left alone to do your work and have enjoyed the supportive feedback of your boss for as long as you can remember. Suddenly, your boss begins nitpicking all your work and doling out frustratingly vague criticisms. Bad sign. "Your boss may have lost confidence in you or is looking for justifications for letting you go," says Dele Lowman Smith, an executive coach in Atlanta. "If your boss's micromanaging is accompanied by constructive recommendations or specific feedback, they more than likely want you to improve," she says. "However, if the criticism is nonspecific, excessive or focused on issues that have little importance, they may be more interested in seeing you leave."

Employees hate to be micromanaged, and to all of a sudden be exposed to that type of management pressure can surely push any employee to look elsewhere. The fact is, it works. While it may not be very *moral*, it's also not *illegal* to begin micromanaging someone. Thus, this unethical tactic to force someone to quit succeeds completely under the radar of the average observer, sometimes even unnoticed by human resources.

b. <u>Excessive documentation</u>: Another tactic closely related to micromanaging is excessive documentation. Of course, you should always document an employee's performance, whether good or bad. Any HR professional will tell you documentation is paramount in the work place. However, when this documentation becomes excessive where it once was very scarce or even non-existent, this could indicate an issue. In that same article mentioned previously, Dominique Rodgers describes a situation like this:

Feedback on your work used to be informal and undocumented, and any mistakes you made were pointed out to you in private, with a friendly talk. Now everything suddenly involves paperwork. You're being asked to fill out timesheets, so the company can keep track of how you spend your hours and minutes; feedback that used to transpire over a coffee break now requires an email chain, with your boss's boss cc'd.

Red flag! As you know, almost every company has a disciplinary process that is implemented when dealing with an underperforming employee, most commonly known as a Performance Improvement Plan or PIP. However, when it comes out of nowhere with no clear reason, something's wrong. Lowman Smith explains it like this:

If the company wants you gone and implements this [Excessive Documentation] with little advance notice, it may be an attempt to psych you out—or a form of intimidation to make you feel insecure or stressed enough to start looking for a new job.

If you think this tactic of documentation is overboard then take a look at the next tactic that is geared towards delivering the same outcome but is engaged from the other end of the spectrum.

c. The Silent Treatment: One of the most common tactics employed to get someone to quit is *The Silent Treatment*. While juvenile in nature, it's very effective and can be wielded by many levels in an organization. It's human nature to want to be liked and appreciated in *any* job, so you can understand the impact it has on someone when, all of a sudden, they are ignored. I'm not just talking about being ignored while passing in the hallway, though that is part of it. I'm talking about no longer being asked to sit in on important meetings, or no longer being assigned to the fun or important projects. Perhaps your normal monthly business travel has been halted, or they are now sending someone else. This silent treatment may not be coming from just one person. Again, Dominique Rodgers adds,

Perhaps the frostiness is coming from your peers too, making the water cooler feel more like a popsicle stand. That could indicate that those colleagues have picked up on your status, as persona non grata, and don't want to become, tainted by association.

In addition to coworkers just keeping their distance, I've seen the silent treatment implemented as a group effort, where the manager holds a small private meeting, enlisting a trusted few to implement his/her plans to oust a target employee.

3. *Unrealistic/Unusual Expectations:* We all have annual performance reviews (or should) where we recap our year's past performance as well as set goals and expectations for the upcoming year. However, when these goals and expectations pop up (sometimes outside a normal annual review) and are well outside the scope of your job or are simply unrealistic, you should begin to take notice. An example might be a salaried employee (not paid hourly) now being asked to put in 50–60 hours a week, including weekends, for no obvious reason, when the normal 40–45 was never an issue. Another example I remember was a human resources manager being tasked by the president of the company with ensuring two senior executives (who hated each other) get along and play nice! That responsibility should rest with the boss of those executives. However, the task was assigned and documented as an new *objective* during an annual performance review for the HR manager. You will witness many other examples throughout your career, but these are all examples of being "set up for failure," a term very well known in *The Executive Arena.*

4. *The Hiring Process Façade*: While this tactic isn't as aggressive or targeted as some of those previously discussed, it is something that is surely actualized and implemented *behind closed doors.* Those who have high *Corporate Political Intelligence* can wrangle their way into being favored or actually landing that promotion or upcoming position. As an example, Joe may be best friends with the president, and the president wants him on board in a newly created role. When this happens, however, there are times when the company must still post the position either internally, publicly or both because of strict company policy. Sometimes it's to simply "save face" with the employees, giving the perception, or presenting the façade, that they are being fair to all possible candidates. Hence the term: Hiring Process Façade. If you are observant, you will see this in corporations that employ unions, but rest assured it does happen to a large degree in traditional organizations as well.

Here's what transpires in a nutshell. A new position becomes available. Who will fill that position has already been decided through unconventional channels, behind closed doors. However, because of the previously mentioned obstacles, the position is posted and the façade of "Please apply if you are interested" is launched. Some of the signs that this may be just a façade are:

1. The position is filled very quickly: We all know that when you are trying to find the right candidate, you make sure you interview enough candidates to ensure you are getting a good sample of the talent pool available.

However, when the position is filled quickly, it could be a sign that the person to fill the position has already been selected.

2. Quick interviews: The average interview takes at least thirty to forty-five minutes. Frankly, if you are a good candidate, it should be over an hour. Any shorter, and there's a good possibility that you are not a good fit, or you just didn't connect with the interviewer. In the case of the hiring façade, the interviews tend to be even quicker. If you realize most interviews are around five to ten minutes long, you can be confident management already has a candidate in mind.

3. Heard it through the grapevine: If you possess strong *Corporate Political Intelligence* (and you will after applying what you've learned in this book), you will most likely be included in, or at the very least be aware of, the hiring façade currently in play. Sometimes word does get out, most times leaked by someone who should have kept their mouth shut. Either way, you may hear chatter about who will get the new position like, "I heard Barry's best friend is going to get the job," or words to that effect. This type of office gossip sometimes has some validity. Something sparked that fire and fueled the gossip, so be perceptive. Knowing who is doing the interviewing and who has the power to make the final decision is critical information, as it could become a vital source pertaining to your own career in the not-so-distant future.

> **Executive Arena Rule:** The very people *in the know*, pertaining to the hiring façade, are the very same people *you* need to build a strong relationship with.

You Have Two Choices: Thus far we have discussed what sometimes goes on behind closed doors. You now have a good understanding of the sometimes devious tactics that can occur to those around us. But what if we find ourselves caught up in certain situations, thus becoming the target of these covert stratagems? What should you do if you are the target of lead control, or the silent treatment? How do you save your job if the company wants you to quit? Should you even try to save your job?

Up to now, the entire purpose of this book is to put you ahead of the game in corporate politics. Having strong *Corporate Political Intelligence* allows you to take a proactive approach to the furtherance of your career, versus being reactive and on the defensive. Nevertheless, however good you are, there is always someone better. There will be times when, because of corporate restructure, mergers, etc., you may fall victim to some of the very things we have been discussing. Perhaps a colleague feels threatened by you and it just so happens he/she has more influence at the current company than you do. Whatever the reason, it is possible that one day you will become the target. So, what is one to do? What actions should you take if you feel the company or some superior wants to get rid of you? What should you do if, all of a sudden, the decent leads you used to get are now going to the new guy? The answer is very simple. You have two choices. Either confront the situation directly or leave the company. Period. Now, before you freak out on me, let's take a look at each option in detail.

1. *Confront the Situation*: If, unfortunately, you become the target of one or more of these "shunning" or "outing"

tactics, the best thing to do is confront the situation directly. I want to be clear about something here. Notice I said, *directly*! In other words, if your supervisor is the source of said tactics, then you should have a heart-to-heart, face-to-face meeting with that person. *Do not*, under any circumstances, run off and complain to HR, your boss's boss, or anyone else about how you believe you are being treated unfairly ... at least, not at first. All that will do is send a strong perceptional message to everyone that you are either a trouble maker, a complainer, or whatever else can be construed from your actions. Instead, sit down with the person you feel is the source—let's call them "the source" for the purpose of this discussion—and have a conversation. This does a couple things for you. Firstly, by not going to HR or anyone else, you are showing the source that, one, you are a cool character, and, two, you could have and could still go above their head, but you chose to have a conversation instead. You see, the source doesn't know you won't eventually go to HR or to their boss, so it gives you the upper hand in trying to resolve the issue. It projects the message that you still have some loyalty to the source, putting you in a more advantageous position towards conflict resolution.

To make the best of your conversation, you must have the source's undivided attention. So don't approach them "in passing" or in the cafeteria. I'd suggest setting up a meeting or appointment so you can have a conversation in private. Secondly, don't combine your conversation with another already regularly scheduled meeting. In other words, don't go into your weekly recap meeting and say, "Excuse me, before we get started, I have something to discuss …" This is important to you and the source, so treat it as such and give it the time and respect it deserves. Again, it all has to do with *Perceptional Messaging*. Do you see where I'm going here?

When you are finally ready to have the discussion, the easiest way to go about it is to just be direct, be honest, yet unassertive. Don't go in guns blazing. *Approach the conversation as if you are seeking a resolution that will benefit both involved*, which, quite frankly, you are! As an example, let's pretend that you know for a fact the quality leads you used to get are now being fed to someone else. You feel the manager wants you out, and you will have a very difficult time hitting your goals unless something changes. I would open the conversation with something like this: "Hey, David, thank you for taking the time to meet with me. I do appreciate it. Look, I just want to be very open and honest here. I'm not sure if I have done something wrong, or if something has changed, but I've noticed I'm no longer being forwarded the same quality leads I normally get. In fact, the amount has dropped off significantly, and it's having an impact on my performance. I don't know if it's something I did, or it's something I caused, but whatever the reason, *I'd like to know what I can do to fix it*." Then, shut up! Let the source respond. Notice the approach was all about what *you* may have done, and how *you* can fix it. Going in with a finger-pointing approach, complaining etc., is never the best tactic.

How they respond depends on the person and the situation. I'm not going to assume what they may or may not say, because it's irrelevant. What I will tell you, is this: if you are direct, professional and go in with an open mind, you will know where you stand when you leave that person's office. Whether they outright deny your claims, blow you off, or actually agree with you and give you solid reasons why your lead flow has been reduced, the ball is now in their court. From a political standpoint you have brought attention to the fact that you *know* what's going on, which basically disarms the source, if only temporarily. Let's face it, you could be wrong in your assumptions about the leads, or maybe there was a mistake in the distribution process. When you take the approach I have described, it allows you to save face and not embarrass yourself in the event you interpreted the situation incorrectly. Imagine, for a moment, if your first reaction was to run off to HR, guns blazing, and bitching to everyone about how you feel. And you were wrong. This would ensure your exit from the company, and not in any positive light. Using *Corporate Political Intelligence* gives you time to analyze the situation, know where you stand, and to decide if you want to let it go, or move on to option number two.

2. *Leave the Company*: More often than not (I'm talking 99% of the time if you want a statistic), once a company or the powers that be decide it's time for a specific employee to go bye-bye, it's going to happen. If, unfortunately, that employee happens to be you, then you need to take specific actions to protect your career. Let me say that again more clearly. You need to take specific actions that will protect you, your family and your career. Notice I didn't say take actions to protect your job, or position, or even your feelings. Please forgive me, because I'm going to be a little "in your face" when I say this because it's important. *If a company doesn't want you around, whether*

justified or not, why would you want to stay? The worst thing you can do in this situation is adopt a "get even" attitude and try to *stick it to them* because you're angry. This isn't about your current company or your ego, this is about your *long-term career and success*! Let's say, for the sake of argument, the example we used previously turned out to be true. They want you gone. But now that you have directly brought up the fact that you know what they are doing, this should buy you plenty of time to seek out a new opportunity. From a career standpoint, or, more specifically, your employment record, you *do not* want to be fired. If you can find a new position, preferably better than the last one, and can peacefully resign, it's better for everyone. Who wants to work at a company where they are not wanted or appreciated?

The reason most people in these situations will run off to HR or begin causing trouble is because of ego. It's because they are too proud or too stupid to realize it's just not worth it. Why waste your valuable energy and talents at a place where they won't be recognized? I'm not saying quit and walk out without securing another opportunity first. That would be silly. I'm advising that when you are in this situation, it's almost always best to do what you can to *buy yourself enough time* to find a better opportunity. By complaining in an attempt to "save your job" you may get to stay on for another month, or even three months, but you won't be moving up or getting promoted. Instead, you'll remain employed at a company with an atmosphere that makes you miserable, around people who are inhospitable, until it's convenient for the company to terminate you. Just let it go. It's only a job.

"It's only by saying 'no' that you can concentrate on the things that are really important." (Steve Jobs)

Points to Remember:

1. The *Peter Principle* is a theory originated by Dr. Laurence J. Peter that basically states: "In a hierarchy, much like in a corporate environment, successful employees tend to rise to their highest level of incompetence." However, that principle can be and has been used as a weapon.

2. *Lead Distribution* or *Lead Control* is one of the most common tactics used to get rid a problem employee who works in sales. In most cases, lead distribution is arbitrary, making it very easy for the distributor to "blackball" another employee.

3. *Being Shunned* is the most favored way for a company to rid itself of an unwanted employee. The objective is to employ specific and consistent tactics, to the point where the target (employee) just leaves the company on their own. This includes but is not limited to: micromanagement, excessive documentation, the silent treatment, and unrealistic or unusual expectations.

4. *The Hiring Process Façade* is another *Executive Arena* tactic you will see employed in corporations that have unions, as well as some traditional organizations. Clues that the hiring process façade is possibly being implemented are: quick interviews, the position is filled quickly, or you actually heard it through the grapevine.

5. You should be building strong relationships with very same people that are "in the know" concerning the hiring façade, for they are the influencers that obviously possess the *back-stage passes* you seek.

6. *You have two choices*, if you should fall victim to some of the very things we have been discussing. If the company wants you gone, you can either *confront the situation* directly, and/or *leave the company*. Remember, your number one priority is to protect your *long-term image and career*. Your current job is just that, a job … and it's merely a stepping stone to a better position bringing you closer to your ultimate goal.

Chapter Nine - Your Network Builds Net Worth

Fred, the Walking Talking Rolodex:

There was a short time in my career, and by short I mean less than a year, when I decided to give real estate a shot. I had just been discharged from the navy and I was looking for my next great venture. I knew if you were good and loved *sales*, real estate was an avenue that could yield a significant income. If you joined the right company, it was the same as starting your own business, and there were no caps on the amount of money you could earn. So I signed up for real estate school and took the plunge. I absolutely loved the school and the instructors were magnificent. I was told that the state of Virginia had one of the toughest real estate exams (and bar exams) in the country, and the first-time pass rate was 48%. But here's the kicker: if you failed the test and had to retake it, the pass rate dropped to 38% and it continued to get worse the more times you retook the exam. The moral here was to make sure you passed it the first time. Not only did I ace the school's final exam, I passed the state exam on the first attempt. Now armed with my state license, I joined Caldwell Banker, mainly because of their training incentives and, honestly, I liked the broker I was talking with. If you don't like the person you are working for, why bother? To make a long story even shorter, I did extremely well, selling my first few properties inside of a few months of being on board. I even created a CMA (Competitive Market Analysis) spreadsheet that was so advanced it cut down on the time it took to do a CMA by 80%. It worked so well, it implemented throughout the brokerage I was part of and was taught during the initial agent training to all new agents.

You are probably asking yourself: If I was so successful at real estate, why am I not still doing it, and what is the point of this story? To answer your questions, while I was very good at selling real estate, the fact is I hated it. Yep, I hated selling real estate. I hated it because my success, while it was technically "my own business," was greatly influenced by the performance of other agents. Both buying and selling agents, almost always from other companies, had to work together to bring any deal to a close. I hated dealing with other agents who did not have the same dedication as me. For the most part, they were part-timers, or they thought because of all the HGTV programs they watched about real estate, it was a fun job that had nothing to do with sales. Unfortunately, it has *everything* to do with sales. Most of the agents I met got into real estate to "make a few extra bucks on the side" and they never really understood that to really be successful in real estate you had to treat it as a full-time sales career. And while you didn't have to have an initial investment of $150,000 as you would in a traditional franchise or other business start-up, you had better treat your real estate business as if you did invest that amount or it was doomed to fail.

To answer the second question—why am I telling you this story?—it comes down to a very valuable lesson I *did* learn while in real estate long ago. It's one of those lessons you always knew deep down inside was important, but never really knew just how important until it smacked you in the face. That lesson is this: *your network builds your net worth.* That's right, the one thing that really hit home was the *network* you need to build and keep building throughout your career, regardless of your chosen vocation.

I was out to lunch with a senior real estate agent who was also my instructor at the time. Let's call him Fred. We hit it off after the whole CMA spreadsheet creation thing and eventually became good friends. He even helped me purchase my first home back in the day. While we were sitting enjoying our lunch, he got a phone call that, from my end, went something like this:

"Hey, Gerald, what can I do for you?" Long pause. "Yes, let me look it up for you," he continued as he placed the caller on speaker and began to scroll through his phone contacts. "It's A1 Cleaners, his number is ..." and Fred gave him the number for what I'm guessing was a recommended dry cleaner.

When he got off the phone, I asked, "I'm guessing that's a past client?"

"Not yet," Fred replied. "One of my actual clients gave him my number because he was looking for a good dry cleaner."

Confused, I asked, "What, are you like the neighborhood Yellow Pages?"

"In a way, yes," he answered, "and that's the idea. I keep a huge contact list of all the local businesses I've dealt with in the area, as well as past clients and other people I've met throughout my career."

"But why?" I asked, now confused even more.

Fred explained, "I purposely want to be the *go-to* person for whatever their need may be." Realizing that I still didn't completely understand where he was coming from, Fred took a sip of his beer, set his glass down, leaned across the table and said softly and slowly, "If all these people are coming to me for all their daily needs, who do you think they will call or recommend when it comes time to buy or sell a property?"

The lightbulb went on immediately, and it became a conversation I will never forget. Remember the lesson we discussed earlier about being considered an expert in your chosen vocation? Well, in this case Fred took that concept to a whole new level. He became a walking-talking Rolodex. If you don't know what a Rolodex is, it's fair to assume you *do* know how to use Google, so look it up. The point here is, Fred was brilliant. He became the go-to guy whenever someone in the community needed a recommendation. Be it a contractor, lawn service, A/C repair, or, in this case a dry cleaner, Fred was the guy to call. He was *Angie's List* in physical form. Think about it this way. Should Fred ever decide to switch jobs or careers, he has a huge contact list at his disposal to either help him land a new position, or, at the very least, it's a list to begin marketing a new product or service to immediately. And guess what? Everyone on that list already trusts him. It's a win-win! So, if you haven't already, start building your list of contacts today.

Using Technology to Build a Network:

LinkedIn: There are so many apps and other software programs designed to help you build a database of contacts; too many to list here. However, *LinkedIn*, as mentioned in a previous chapter, is a good place to start. Not only did we discuss it in a previous chapter, we have all heard of LinkedIn as it's literally the most popular social media platform when it comes to *business contacts*. While Facebook is, of course, number one, when it comes to strictly business-related connections, LinkedIn is perfect and very easy to use. Your goal should be to at least reach a minimum of 500 first-level contacts as this will provide you with a baseline for connecting with other first-, second-, and even third-level contacts all over the world. LinkedIn also offers a premium membership at a cost of around $30 to up to $99 a month, depending on the plan you choose if you are looking for more options. These memberships provide different services, such as to assist you with hiring and job searches as well, and being able to contact people on LinkedIn, even if you are not "connected" to them.

Basic LinkedIn is free and does a superb job in helping you build a large network of business contacts in its original form, so take advantage of it.

ScanBizCards: Since we are always on the go, *ScanBizCards* is another great app available for free in a *Lite* version, or for a few bucks you can get the full pro version. It's available in the App Store or just about anywhere for any smartphone.

No one wants to keep a giant stack of business cards anymore, but the fact is, even in this wonderful age of technology, handing out these pieces of cardboard isn't going away anytime soon. However, now when someone hands you their business card, you simply take a picture of it, and ScanBizCards automatically pulls the information from the card and populates your contacts lists. You no longer have to type in the information manually. It also saves the actual image of the business card, so it's easy to share the info with others. The app also has what it calls *email capture*, where it scans emails you receive and captures the email signatures that a lot of emails contain, converting them into business contacts for you. I use this app and highly recommend you download a copy and start using it as soon as you can. There are a lot of similar apps available, but I believe ScanBizCards is one of the best.

It's always about who you know:

We have all heard the phrase "It's not what you know, it's who you know." I admit there is a lot of controversy around that phrase as it implies you can get hired for a position because you are related to the owner, or some other kind of favoritism. People who believe that haven't a clue what *networking* is all about, and the value it can have in building a successful career in *The Executive Arena*. I'm here to tell you, it *is* about who you know, but, more importantly, it's also about *who knows you*!

For example, just because a position isn't advertised with *CareerBuilder*, *Indeed* or on a company's website, doesn't mean an open position doesn't exist. Some of the best positions available today go unadvertised, especially when you're talking about higher level management positions. Perhaps it's just a mid-level position and the company needs to replace someone and they either want to keep it quiet, or they don't want to spend the money to advertise. Whatever the reason, having an inside track to some of these available positions can prove extremely valuable. Almost every mid-level to senior management position I have been hired for was not publicly posted or otherwise advertised. I landed these opportunities through the relationships formed from building a network. I remember specifically a prior boss calling me and inviting me and my wife to dinner, to discuss a new opportunity for a start-up company he was now working for. In another example, a previous employee, without me knowing, recommended me to her current company president when she heard they were looking for a vice president of sales and marketing. I accepted the positions, both of which turned out to be wonderful opportunities! So a network should not be considered a "nice thing to have." It is a mandatory tool in your *Executive Arena* toolbox that you should take very seriously. What's more, it doesn't cost you a penny to begin building your network right now! In fact, you probably already have a good-sized pool to begin pulling from as we speak.

Start with opening a LinkedIn account and begin scrolling through the "recommendations" LinkedIn will give you every time you log on. The recommendations they present are the first level connections of those people you are already connected with. If you request a connection from them, most will accept your request. I would also recommend you spend time daily scrolling through the different posts and articles and share the ones you like. In short, *be active* on LinkedIn.

You can also take a look at your Facebook connections, and if they are professionals you'd like to be connected with, then search for them on LinkedIn and send off a connection request.

Additionally, and I believe the most important thing, do a search on LinkedIn for those in your current industry or chosen vocation. If you are looking to break into a particular industry, search for those people who are already working in that field. For example, if you work in the hospitality industry, you can actually search for other people in that industry by typing "hospitality" in the search bar. Send them a connection request and see if they accept it. You will be pleasantly surprised by how many people will actually accept your request, because they also know the value of building a network. Then, down the road, should the time come for you to search for a new/better position, you can reach out directly to those people for help.

Lastly, make sure you complete your LinkedIn profile. Treat your profile as your professional *public* résumé, because that's exactly what it is. Often, before someone will accept your connection request, they will view your profile, mostly to make sure you are not just trying to sell them something. However, they also view your profile to see if you might be of value to *their* network, either now or in the future. So, take your time when building your profile, and make sure you give it the time and attention it deserves as it will ultimately represent *you* as a professional.

Bridges: to burn or not to burn:

Paul was a senior executive that had worked in the for-profit education industry for many years. While we never worked together, he had been after me to work for his company for a long time. We were first introduced to each other when I applied for a position with his company years prior, but at that time decided it wasn't a good fit. We parted on good terms, and we vowed to stay in touch with each other. A few years down the road, when my family and I were living in North Carolina, we decided to make a move up north and I reached out to Paul to see if there were any opportunities available. Of course, there were, and after a couple weeks of face-to-face meetings over dinner discussing salary negotiations and the like, I accepted a regional director position (or so I thought), and we packed up the family and moved to New England. It was the land of amazing crab legs and lobster at the best prices, all combined with breathtaking views of rocky beaches, historical landmarks and lighthouses! We found a wonderful house to rent in the heart of Manchester, Connecticut, that came with a huge above ground pool, a pool table in the finished basement and a snow blower in the garage that we would surely need come winter. All seemed right in the world. However, after a few short weeks in my new position, I began to realize the job I was doing was not the position I was hired for. What was supposed to be a regional director position (managing multiple locations), had somehow turned into a sales position in a single location. Unbeknownst to me at the time, the company was hurting financially in that region and was on a mission to find great sales people to bring their profits back to acceptable levels. I was to be one of those sales people, until such time they could later give me the region as promised. In their minds, they would call me whatever I wanted as far as title was concerned and pay me a $90k base salary as long as I would directly sell for them. This may not sound like a bad deal to you, but I was very disappointed and angry at the fact I had just relocated my family across the country for a job that didn't really exist.

Nevertheless, I performed as a "sales person," or what the industry calls an admissions rep, and I sold my ass off! I actually broke many monthly performance records, but at the same time as I was smiling and enrolling students, I was also searching for new opportunities. It took only a few months before I found another great opportunity and submitted my resignation. It was a Friday afternoon just before the end of the workday when I submitted the official resignation letter to Paul which I copied to the company president. I stated in the letter that while I deeply appreciated the opportunity to work for them, I didn't feel my current position as a sales person was advantageous to my career and needed to pursue other opportunities. I stated that I would return any company property I had at home (which included a laptop and other things) to the office first thing Monday morning. It was a very professional letter, in which I did not blame or point the finger at anyone or anything and thanked everyone once again for the opportunity to work for them. That was when all hell broke loose! The company (or I thought it was the company) was so pissed off, they had one of their school directors call me personally and request we meet at a local Dunkin Donuts to return the laptop and other things, instead of meeting on Monday morning at the school. At first, I was a bit taken aback by their being so upset that I left that they would treat me like someone who had stolen from the company, completely cutting off any access I may have had to their property and employees. But then I realized what was really going on.

In summary, you may be saying to yourself, "That bridge is now burned," but you would be mistaken. You see, I know for a fact the real reason for their actions was to prevent me from communicating my true reasons for leaving with other employees. And, honestly, I was okay with that, and I'll tell you why. Since I had and always have built loyalty with my peers, many employees of the company reached out to me soon after my departure. You see, it wasn't the company that was upset, it was Paul himself. Of course, the president of the company was disappointed that I left because I was a good employee, but Paul was furious because, if you remember, I directly, in a professional way, called him out. My resignation letter was copied to the president, which stated that my *sales position* was not advantageous to my career. Whatever Paul's motive was for not delivering on his promises, I can assure you it never came up in conversation once I left. As a matter of fact, you should know Paul no longer works for that corporation. But here is the real moral of the story. If any bridges were burned, I didn't light the match. Secondly, the bridge between the company and I was not touched. It was the bridge between Paul and me that was burned to the ground by Paul's own hand.

So regardless of how you feel about a company or how you may perceive they've treated you, never burn that bridge. *People don't leave companies, people leave people*, and while it may feel good to lash out at a company when you feel you've been wronged, I assure you it's not the right thing to do in the long run. More often than not, it's an individual that has caused the situation, and not the company as a whole. More importantly, most industries are very tightly knit. Industries like healthcare, hospitality, education and many others operate in a very small world. In other words, a lot of senior management personnel communicate with each other, even across competitive lines. I've known many at the director and VP level of one company having beers and discussing employee issues with their counterparts at competing companies. Of course, they didn't give up company secrets, but they damn sure shared bad experiences (and good ones as well) they may have had with current and past employees. In short, word gets around, so never ever burn bridges, especially when you are trying to build a strong business network.

If you do your own research on whether or not to burn a bridge, you will find many articles that promote both sides of the argument. Some will say never burn a bridge you may have to cross in the future. Others say, if you have been wronged or mistreated, burn the bridge. Still others insist if you may be tempted to cross that bridge again (that once caused you pain) in the future, it's better to burn it. I say, you need to strongly consider who or what the bridge is actually made from and what the ultimate goal is should you proceed.

Ask yourself these questions:

1. Are you pissed at the company, when, in actuality, it's a single individual that has caused the situation?
2. Are you just making a statement? Will burning the bridge actually help advance your career, or is it an action that will simply make you *feel* better?

3. Is it absolutely necessary to save and or honor your integrity?

Question number 3, I believe, is the *only* reason you should ever consider burning a bridge. Needing to preserve your integrity (not be a show off) is the only acceptable reason for burning a bridge.

Liz Ryan, a forbes.com contributor, in an article titled "Never Burn Bridges - Except in these 5 Cases" writes:

> Burn a bridge when your integrity is at stake and the only alternatives are to burn the bridge, or to do or say something unethical. It happened to Geeta, who was hired as a Quality Control Manager for a start-up company. Geeta was enthusiastic about her new role until she realized that her company hired a Quality Control Manager for show, not because they care about quality control. Geeta was silenced over and over and her testing plans were pushed aside. Defective products streamed out the door while the company made excuses. Finally, Geeta was called to a Senior Staff Meeting where she was called on the carpet for the quality problems. She had to make a choice -- tell the truth about the brick walls she had run into or stay silent and look and feel like an idiot. Geeta told the truth. The senior staff applauded her honesty in the meeting but three days later Geeta was terminated. She was glad to be gone and glad that she'd been honest about the real problems in the company. Soon afterward the CEO was ousted by the Board of Directors. Is Geeta sorry she burned a bridge with that CEO? Not in the slightest!"

In closing, after you review the three questions above, if your decision to burn that bridge was truly honorable, you should have no problem telling another employer proudly, with your head held high, why you did what you did and why you left the company. Then and only then should you set fire to that bridge. Remember: the toes you step on today just might be connected to the ass you'll have to kiss tomorrow.

Points To Remember:

1. *Your network builds your net worth.* You need to build and keep building a network of contacts throughout your career regardless of your chosen vocation, consisting of everyone you meet and do business with.
2. *Become a walking-talking Rolodex.* Be the to go-to guy for your those in your network so they come to *you* for recommendations and solutions to their problems.
3. *Use the technology available* like LinkedIn and ScanBizCards to manage and utilize your network to your advantage.
4. *It's not just who you know, it's who knows you.* Just because a position isn't advertised doesn't mean an open position doesn't exist. Some of the best positions available today go unadvertised, especially when you're talking about higher level management positions.
5. *People don't leave companies, people leave people*, and while it may feel good to lash out at a company when you feel you've been wronged, I assure you it's not the right thing to do in the long run, with the exception of preserving your integrity.

Chapter Ten - Behold your Biggest Asset!

"If you want something bad enough, you'll find a way. If you don't you'll find an excuse." (Jim Rohn)

It is about 8:00 p.m. on New Year's Eve and Dick Clark's *Rockin' Eve 2018* with Ryan Seacrest is playing on the big screen in the family room. My wife and I, along with the kids (while we eat snacks and enjoy our favorite beverage), are printing pictures from our hand-held devices of the things we want to accomplish in the upcoming new year. The night before, we went out to purchase a nicely framed bulletin board that, by midnight, would be transformed into our vision board for the new year. What this "vision board" is will be discussed a little later, but for now I want to focus on something that is absolutely essential to your success. It is the magnet that will bring all these newly acquired skills together. It is the platform from which all your creative ideas will launch and is the fuel for your deepest desires. That something is *you*.

Up until now we have discussed a lot of things that will surely put you on the path to achieving the career you are looking for, but unless it's put into practice, all this knowledge is for nothing. I intentionally brought up New Year's Eve because it's the time when millions of people seemingly reflect on the past year and begin to focus on the upcoming year. Most people, over the holiday season, will begin to announce their New Year's resolutions to their friends and family and promise "this year I will finally give up smoking" or "I will lose 100 pounds" or "I will finish that new book I've been working on" etc., etc. The list goes on and on. And rightly so, because if there is ever a "best time" to set some new goals and make changes, New Year's Eve would be it! But why do so many resolutions fall short a few weeks into the new year, if they even get off the ground at all?

The answer is that most people don't *really* want to go through the challenges and sometimes the pain required to achieve their goals. It's the truth. Look, quitting smoking or losing fifty pounds is not easy. Trust me, I finally quit smoking after thirty-five years of it, and it's tough. But resolutions are abounding and will continue to do so year after year. People just want to feel good about themselves. Who doesn't? That's why so many of us set up these resolutions so haphazardly. Statistics show that of the millions of people who proclaim a major change on 1 January, only 80% ever make it past the six-week mark. More than 95% fail to completely achieve their resolution. That leaves the top 5% once again. They are the ones who set goals and achieve them; those that set a New Year's resolution and follow through. What's the secret? *You*! The secret is *you* have to be ready. *You* have to really want the desired outcome and be prepared for the possible pain and struggles that come with the journey towards achieving that goal, to have any chance of succeeding. *You* must understand what it's going to take to achieve something and focus on those specific tasks to get you there. For example, don't just say, "I'm going to be a better manager." Instead say, "I'm going to be a better manager by doing A, B and C." You've got to focus on the *specific tasks* required to achieve the goal and prepare yourself for the pain and struggle you may endure in completing those tasks!

In December of 2015, Beverly D. Flaxington wrote an article in *Psychology Today* titled, "The 5 Reasons Why New Year's Resolutions Fail." In this article one of the reasons she states is:

> Your resolutions were not properly defined. "I want to travel more," "I am going to be more responsible" and "I will do my job better" are not very good resolutions. They are too vague and don't lead to a specific outcome. In order for them to yield results, your New Year's resolutions, and any other goals that you might have, need to be S.M.A.R.T. (specific, measurable, achievable, realistic and time-bound).

Another reason, she writes, is:

> You didn't have the right mindset. Wanting something and working towards getting it are two fundamentally different things. It can be difficult to focus on fulfilling a resolution when you are not in a good place in your life. For instance, last year you wanted to take on more responsibilities at work, but your mind was constantly preoccupied with troubles at home, or you decided to quit smoking but didn't make an effort to avoid temptations, so after a week's time you relapsed into

the old habits. If you are not mentally prepared for all the hard work, distractions, and setbacks that might be ahead of you, you will most likely fail.

As you can see, *you* have to be in the right frame of mind. You have to be ready and willing to change *inside* to invoke action and change on the *outside*. Simply put, you have to be *ready* for success. You must be ready for what life may throw at you, at that moment when you are just about to cross the finish line. Ready for the obstacles and setbacks that will surely take other less-prepared players out of the game. So, in this chapter, we will focus entirely on you and what *you* can do to ensure you are prepared, both mentally and physically, for the challenge, the change and the success that comes with it! For *you* are your greatest asset.

Know your Goals, Share Your Ambitions

I was attending a huge four-day networking conference in Atlanta, Georgia, where people from all over the country came together to learn about how to promote and grow their own business. If you have ever experienced one of these large conferences, with companies like Mary Kay, Pampered Chef, even Subway, LegalShield and the like, you know that the energy that permeates these convention centers is addictive and energizing. Everyone in attendance is on a mission, pumped and ready to take on the world. It was the last night of the conference, and I headed down to the lounge for a quick bite and a cocktail. I pulled up a seat at the bar and, as luck would have it, Jim—let's call him that—who happened to be the keynote speaker earlier that evening, casually walked in and sat right next to me at the bar. I had been a huge fan of his writings and teachings for years so, honestly, I felt as if

I had just won the lottery. A crowd of people, trying not to seem obvious, followed him into the lounge and were now hovering around us like a bunch of bees trying to pollinate. They were just as excited as I was, all wanting a few minutes of personal time in the hope that some additional knowledge or "industry secret" might be bestowed upon them. Of course, I had the best seat in the house, so, unless I scared him off, he was all mine.

As others constantly came up to shake his hand or ask him for an autograph, which he graciously provided, I knew I needed to draw his attention, without coming off like just another star-struck bumble bee. When there seemed to be a break in the action, and Jim finally placed his order with the bartender, it was my chance. I told the bartender to put Jim's drink on my tab.

Jim looked over with a smile and said, "Thank you, I appreciate it."

I nodded and then replied with, "Do you ever get used to the crowds following you?"

Jim chuckled and looked over at me with a big smile. "Nope," he said, very matter-of-fact, "but I embrace it. It's a constant reminder that I'm heading in the right direction, that I'm fulfilling my purpose." He held up his glass, waiting for me to lift mine.

Understanding his message and his words, I raised my glass. "Cheers," I said as we tapped our glasses together.

> **Executive Arena Rule:** When you are confident in your purpose and direction, you exert a positive *energy* that is contagious and magnetizing.

Jim and I talked for almost two hours about the importance of knowing what you want. About having a clear image of not only *what* you want to achieve in detail, but *why* you want to achieve it. He called it *knowing your why*. We discussed our "whys" and a few other things that we both agreed were instrumental in achieving success. Coincidentally, nothing we spoke about was anything new or revolutionary. These success principles have been around for centuries, but most people (the 95%) simply fail to realize their significance, or they just toss it out as hogwash. They simply don't believe these principles can have that much of an impact, and thus impose their own limitations. So, let's talk about getting specific on *your* goals and ambitions. Let's discuss the five principles that will help you become clear about what you want, and why you want it, so you too can exert a contagious, magnetic positive energy.

1. **Have a vision with purpose**: Who wouldn't like to have more money or a better career or own a yacht or own a beach house in the Florida Keys? I'm not saying wanting these material things is bad. In fact, it's great to want to be a millionaire and have all these great physical possessions. However, acquiring these goods cannot be the sole purpose of your venture. In other words, Jim Rohn said, to make a fortune, you must "find a way to bring more value to the market, by being a servant to others." For example, the reason I'm writing this book, my purpose, is to help aspiring executives reach their

goals, and to do so faster than I did, by hopefully shortening their learning curve. My purpose is to level the playing field and teach to those new to the corporate world what it took me years to learn. If they can bypass the mistakes I made and achieve their goals, whereas without this book they would not—or, at the very least, it would take them much longer—then I have *added value to the marketplac*e. The book sales, the notoriety, the money that comes from publishing this book is a *byproduct of my purpose, it's not the actual purpose.* What is the purpose behind your goal? In one of Napoleon Hill's great books, *How to Raise Your Own Salary,* he interviews Mr. Andrew Carnegie where he outlines the seventeen success principles. This book is the actual transcript of that interview between these two great successes. This is the interview that took place *before* Hill ever wrote *Think and Grow Rich.* It's a fantastic read and I highly suggest you get a copy for yourself. I believe it's his best book ever because you hear these success principles directly from the source with no filtration or another's interpretation. In this book Andrew Carnegie speaks of the first and *most important* success principle. He called it *Definiteness of Purpose.* During this discussion, Mr Carnegie states,

> Study any person who is known to be a permanent success and you will find that he has a Definite Major Goal; he has a plan for the attainment of this goal; he devotes the major portion of his thoughts and his efforts to the attainment of this purpose.

In summary, one of the things Mr. Carnegie is saying is that you must have a *clear* goal in mind and the goal must have a moral purpose! Your plan to bring value to the market place must be your *mission* in life! All the other things that comes along with being successful are merely the *result* of achieving your ultimate goal/purpose.

> **Executive Arena Rule:** Any goals you launch that focus purely on acquiring material things do not have the fuel needed to complete the journey.

I will leave you with this final note: "One doesn't become wealthy because their goal was to become wealthy. One becomes wealthy because they bring a *Wealth of Value* to the marketplace" (Richard Spector). What is the purpose behind your goal? What value do you want to bring to the marketplace? How do you want to make the world a better place?

2. **Create a Vision Board**: Now that you hopefully understand and have outlined your *vision with purpose*, the fun can really begin. Previously we discussed the importance of not focusing on the material things. That when you are building your vision with purpose rocket, you should focus on the value you can bring to the market, not all the cool stuff that may come along with being successful. Well, now it's time to shift gears. The rocket is your purpose, and it's ready to launch. But now you must generate the fuel to power the damn thing! To achieve this, we must master a technique called *visualization*.

Earlier I spoke about New Year's Eve and our tradition of creating a *vision board* for the new year. So what exactly is a vision board? There is an example of our 2018 vision board on the ArenaTrilogy.com website. It's basically a piece of large poster board, or, preferably, cork or bulletin board, where you can print and/or cut out and place pictures from a magazine, newspaper or the internet on the board that represent the things you want to achieve. Here is where you want to build a visual representation of the lifestyle you want to achieve by filling your vision with purpose! Our vision board had pictures of the now owned Annual Family Premium Passes to Universal Studios in Florida. We had pictures of the Tesla Model X vehicle, and even pictures of Italy, Australia, and India, representing world travel. I even put up a picture that said "National Best Seller," because I wanted my books to reach millions. There are no wrong answers to how your vision board will look.

Jack Canfield, award winning author of *Chicken Soup for the Soul*, and one of the best motivational speakers and teachers of the *Law of Attraction* writes:

Also known as dream boards, these simple devices are one of the most valuable visualization tools available to you. The inspirational collages serve as your image of the future – a tangible example, idea or representation of where you are going. They should represent your dreams, your goals, and your ideal life. Your brain will work tirelessly to achieve the statements you give your subconscious mind. And when those statements are the affirmations and images of your goals, you are destined to achieve them! By representing your goals with pictures and images you will actually strengthen and stimulate your emotions because your mind responds strongly to visual stimulation... and your emotions are the vibrational energy that activates the Law of Attraction. The saying: "A picture is worth a thousand words," certainly holds true here. If you have already defined your dreams, it's time to illustrate them visually.

Once the vision board is complete it should be displayed where you will see it every day as a constant reminder of your goals! Some people put it in their bedroom, so it remains kind of private, but I don't agree with that. We placed ours in the kitchen where you couldn't help but notice it as soon as you walked through the door. I *want* someone to ask, "What is this?" which forces me to explain it, as well as publicly announce my dreams and ambitions. I don't have a problem with that. Nor should you because one should be confident and proud of what they want and where they are going in life. Again, it's the same reason you should tell everyone you know that you are going to quit smoking. It really applies peer pressure (in a good way) and forces you to follow through. Think about it this way: If you are afraid or embarrassed about what people will think of this vision board or the goals you have displayed on it, then what does that say about your true convictions about achieving those goals? Moreover, if you don't tell anyone about your goals and dreams, and you fall short, where's the blowback? Who's going to say, "Hey, how is that quitting smoking project coming along?" So tell people what your goals are, and don't listen to those who tell you to keep them to yourself. This brings me to our next principle.

3. **Announce Your Goals and Ambitions**: The biggest mistake employees make is assuming the company or their boss *knows* or "should know" they want to make more money, or that they want a promotion or to even someday run the damn company. Still to this day I'm amazed at how many people have said to me, "I've worked for this company for years, and I have never received a raise," but when I ask them if they have ever asked for one, they almost always say *no*. I mean seriously? If you want a raise or you want to be considered for a promotion, you have to make sure you make your desires known to those who can deliver it. In summary, it's all about *proactive communication*. Earlier in the book when we discussed *Perceptional Messaging*, we were talking about a subtler approach or a more passive type communication. However, when it comes to your goals and ambitions, specifically raises and promotions, you need a more direct approach. Here are a few things you can do to ensure that next raise or promotion:

   a. *Announce your accomplishments* (big or small). For example, let's say on Monday your boss asked you to create a detailed report, to be completed and delivered to her by Friday. You jump on it and complete it on Wednesday. You attach the report to an email that reads: "Here is the report you wanted. Let me know if you need anything else. - Sally." That did absolutely nothing towards announcing your accomplishments. Sure, you did send it in a few days early, and perhaps your boss did notice that fact. However, never assume! You should still make note of the fact, but not in a way that comes across as bragging or boastful. I would write something like this: "Here is the completed report you requested. I hope you don't mind it a few days early. :) If you need anything else or have any revisions, we have plenty of time before the Friday deadline, so let me know. - Sally." Notice the difference in these two email examples? Not only did we make it known the report was in early, we did so in a way that came across as being a proactive team player, not boisterous. This is a skill you should master and make habitual as you progress throughout your career.

b. *Discuss your goals with the influencers.* Another principle we need to discuss is ensuring those around you (of importance) are aware of your goals and ambitions. Again, assuming the powers-that-be know your intentions is simply that, an assumption. Even in casual conversation over a cocktail it's okay, and, frankly, recommended, to let people know, for example, that one day you hope to be in charge of your own advertising or marketing department, or you want to be a vice president because you have some great ideas to help the company. It's also good to get feedback towards achieving that goal. Remember previously we talked about selecting and using a confidant? Well, in this case, especially if your confidant is also your boss, I would highly recommend you ask them for help in achieving your next position. In July of 2016, Elana Lyn Gross, a Forbes.com contributor, wrote an article called "Managers Share the Best Ways to Ask for a Raise (and get it)." In this article she quotes

Danielle Harlan, PhD, the founder and CEO of The Center for Advancing Leadership and Human Potential. Dr. Harlen states:

Have an honest and open conversation with your manager. If you've been in your current role for at least six months, then in a non-pushy or self-serving way, have a conversation with your supervisor to let them know that, while your first priority is to excel in your current role, your long-term goal is to advance and that you want to make sure you're doing everything that you can to set yourself up for success.

She goes on to say to ask your manager for their recommendations on how you can improve in your current role and what you can do to position yourself well for the next role. If you remember, this is exactly what I asked Kevin for when I set up those monthly one-on-one meetings with him. Coincidentally, it was he who gave me my first promotion from a director to vice president. So, share your goals and ambitions, and don't be afraid to have simple, honest face-to-face conversations.

4. **Write Down Your Goals**: What if there was a secret power that would greatly increase your chances of being a success? What if this power did not cost you anything to implement, with the exception of about twenty to thirty minutes of your time periodically. And what if employing this secret power was not only easy, it was actually something fun to do? Would you use it? Before you answer that question and kid yourself, let me explain something to you. The simple process of writing down

your goals can and will have a huge impact on achieving them. It's so easy to do, yet, unfortunately, the majority of us never bother to put our dreams in writing.

> **Executive Arena Rule**: The major difference between a pipe dream and a goal? One is in writing, the other is not.

If writing down your goals can really have that much of a positive impact, why don't more people do it? I'll refer you back to Jeff Olson's book *The Slight Edge*, or the teachings of Jim Rohn, or any of the other greats out there. I myself have taught this numerous times. If something is very easy to do, it's also very easy *not* to do it. Furthermore, for some reason, most people believe that if a task or process is easy or minuscule, then its impact or effect must also be minuscule, but that's simply not true. Think about what we have been discussing throughout this book, particularly when it comes to *Perceptional Messaging*. The little things *do matter* and that, my friend, is the *real* secret to success.

International speaker, best-selling author, and consultant for over three decades, Mary Morrissey, wrote an article in huffingtonpost.com titled "The Power of Writing Down Your Goals and Dreams." She writes:

> Dr. Gail Matthews, a psychology professor at the Dominican University in California, recently studied the art and science of goal setting. She gathered two hundred and sixty-seven people together — men and women from all over the world, and from all walks of life, including entrepreneurs, educators, healthcare professionals, artists, lawyers and bankers. She divided

the participants into groups, according to who wrote down their goals and dreams, and who didn't. She discovered that those who wrote down their goals and dreams on a regular basis achieved those desires at *a significantly higher level than those who did not.* In fact, she found that you become 42% more likely to achieve your goals and dreams, simply by writing them down on a regular basis. The likelihood that you'll transform your desires into reality goes up even further if you *share your written goals* with a friend who believes in your ability to succeed.

An often discussed 1979 Harvard survey of a class of MBA program students asked, "Have you set clear, written goals for your future and made plans to accomplish them?" Here's what the study revealed: 3% in the class had written goals and plans, 13% had just unwritten goals, and the remaining 84% had no goals at all.

Ten years later, the 3% of individuals with written goals had a higher net worth than the other 97% combined! To be exact, the 13% with goals earned twice as much as the 84% with no goals. Even more incredible, the 3% with *written goals and plans* earned about ten times as much as the others.

The 1979 Harvard survey is a little controversial, because some have claimed there is no evidence of the survey, but I'm guessing the claimants were people who never wrote down their goals, so they're a little upset to begin with. Regardless, you can't argue with the fact that simply writing down your goals can help in a big way towards achieving success. It helps you articulate your goals by putting them down on paper, it costs absolutely nothing monetarily, and it can be fun! There is no downside, and it will help keep you focused on the task at hand (achieving success) while navigating *The Executive Arena*. So, do it … *today!*

5. **Have an Attitude of Gratitude**: Most say once they get the nice house, the nice cars, the great relationship, the big bank account, *then* they will happy! They go through life busting their asses, trying to reach that "final destination" where they will "finally have all the money they want" to travel, or buy the cool toys they want and live happily ever after. Well, most people have that backwards. The top 5% knows and has always known that if you are *happy first*, happy and grateful *now* for the things you have and the life you have, the other things will come to you. By being a positive force of happy and grateful energy, you can't help but attract more things into your life that will make you happy and grateful. The opposite is also true.

You may be saying to yourself, "I can't be grateful right now because I have nothing to be grateful for." Perhaps you've had some hard times; perhaps you've been fired from your job; or you feel you came from a dysfunctional family and never got the opportunity others have gotten. Maybe you are just not happy with where you are in your career, which is one reason you are reading this book. By focusing on the negatives in your life, you will surely attract more things into your life to be miserable about. Whatever your situation, you can begin to change your results by changing your attitude. It's called having an *attitude of gratitude*, and it's a skill you should begin to practice, until it becomes a habit.

Everyone can think of many things to be grateful for, regardless of your situation. You can be grateful for your health, or that your kids are doing great in school. You can be grateful that you have a job, even though it's not your dream job yet. You can be grateful for your pets, your clothes, even the fact that you have fresh running water and air conditioning. Trust me, in southern Florida, AC is about as important as oxygen. You get the picture. Here are some tips to help you towards developing an attitude of gratitude:

1. *Keep a Gratitude Journal:* Here we go again with writing things down. Are you beginning to see a pattern here? Keep a journal on your nightstand and every morning when you get up, or evening before you go to bed, write down a few things you were grateful for that day. Maybe that traffic was light, or something bigger, like you got a raise. The point here is that you are conditioning your mind to focus on the positive, while staying away from the negative thoughts that can really bring you down.

2. *Have a Gratitude Trigger:* Pick something you like that will give you a subtle reminder to be grateful. In a best-selling book and movie called *The Secret* by Rhonda Byrne, she and many of her guest speakers, all experts in the Law of Attraction, discuss the importance of expressing gratitude and having a reminder to keep you in that *attitude of gratitude*. One gentleman speaks of having what he calls a *gratitude rock*. It's simply a special rock he found down at a stream that he keeps in his pocket. Each time he reaches into his pocket, he feels the rock, and it

reminds him to think of something he can be grateful for. At the end of the day when he empties his pockets and puts his keys and change on top his dresser, he sees the rock, and, again, thinks of something he can be grateful for. Your trigger can be anything, not just something physical you hold in your pocket. Some use a favorite color or an animal or word. Anytime they encounter their trigger, either seen, spelled out or spoken, they think *gratitude*. I use "gold." Whenever I see a gold-plated statue, the word "gold" or even gold jewelry, it reminds me to be grateful. You should see what happens when I walk into a jewelry store! It doesn't matter what your trigger is, just have one. It helps you to be more alert and attuned to the Law of Attraction and having an *attitude of gratitude*.

3. *Share Your Gratitude*: If you have an employee or even a coworker that performs well on a project, or just does a great overall job, let them know how grateful you are to have them on your team. Don't be afraid to share the things you are grateful for with others. This brings those in your charge and around you in the work place closer to you, builds loyalty and trust, thus making you a more effective leader and much more approachable.

Lindsay Holmes from huffingtonpost.com writes in an article titled "The 10 Things Grateful People Do Differently": "Ralph Waldo Emerson once said that in order to achieve contentment, one should cultivate the habit of being grateful for every good thing that comes to you, and toggle thanks continuously." Emerson, who explored the meaning of a good life in much of his work, wasn't far off when it comes to what we now know about counting our blessings. Research is continually finding that expressing thanks can lead to a healthier, happier and less stressed lifestyle. "Life is a series of problems that have to be solved, and a lot of times those problems cause stress," Robert Emmons, a gratitude researcher and psychology professor at the University of California, told *Huffington Post*. "Gratitude can be that stress buster." So, practice and perfect an attitude of gratitude, for it will improve your lifestyle and make you a better person.

Personal Development - Becoming a Life-long Student of Self-Improvement

"Work hard at your job and you'll make a decent living. Work hard on yourself, and you'll make a fortune!" (Jim Rohn)

Those words from world-renowned and award-winning motivational speaker and author Jim Rohn have had more impact on my life than anything else. They are the basis for all other learning and encompass the meaning and purpose behind *The Executive Arena*. As we have already mentioned so many times, being good at your job is only half the battle. The other half, if you are to be truly successful, rests within you. You have to become a better communicator. You have to become a more effective leader. You have to become a master at *Corporate Political Intelligence* and *Perceptional Messaging*. All these skills are about *you* improving as a person, a colleague, and a leader. It's not about you being an electrician, a banker an engineer or even an astronaut.

So what exactly is personal development? Not to be confused with professional development, the standard definition is: personal development covers activities that improve awareness and identity, develop talents and potential, build human capital, enhance the quality of life and contribute to the realization of dreams and aspirations. In short, it's a life-long process of continued learning that's designed to make *you* a better person! Most companies will support continuing education relating to one's specific job, for example annual seminars covering the new employment laws going into effect, or the new tax laws for the upcoming year. Unfortunately, most corporations won't support much that relates to your *personal* growth. Only a handful of company leaders know the value of continued *personal* development. So, once again, it's up to you to take control. And who better to have that responsibility?

Let's discuss some of the best known methods for personal development that I use on a regular basis:

1. **Meditation:** Meditation has been scientifically proven to have an abundance of physical health benefits. Daily meditation can relieve stress, lower blood pressure, help fight addictions, enhance sleep and so much more. What exactly is meditation? Is it sitting in a Buddha-like position for hours with your thumbs and "screw you" fingers touching oh so slightly? Well, not exactly. In fact, meditation can be as quick as a five- to ten-minute exercise where you focus entirely on your breathing. Merriam-Webster.com defines meditation as:

   a. To engage in contemplation or reflection, (he *meditated* long and hard before announcing his decision).

   b. To engage in mental exercise (such as concentration on one's breathing or repetition of a mantra) for the purpose of reaching a heightened level of spiritual awareness.

However, meditation is so much more.

> **Executive Arena Rule:** Meditation is a conscious practice of informing and instructing the subconscious mind to deliver a desired outcome or manifestation.

In other words, you are meditating on what you want to achieve in life. It's another way of clearly identifying your goals and ambitions, but instead of writing them down on paper, they're going directly to your subconscious mind. Now here is the kicker: when you combine *meditation* with *visualization*, the power you can wield is immeasurable.

It was 1987 and I was only twenty-two years old, serving on board the USS *Forrestal* CV-59, an aircraft carrier stationed in Mayport Naval Station, Florida. After only a little over three years in the navy, I had recently been promoted to Petty Officer 2nd Class (E-5), which was pretty quick compared to other ratings (job classifications) in the navy. We were currently coming to the end of a short deployment (about week four of five) when I was called up to the radio room for a phone call. This does not normally happen to any average enlisted sailor, especially to a *snipe*, which is slang for someone who works in engineering far below the waterline. A call like this would normally mean there is a death in the family, or something even more serious. I was shaking so badly I could hardly focus on where I was going. As I made my way towards "officers' country" up the endless steel stairs (ladders), hatches and hallways, each level became more comfortable from the air conditioning and the deck shinier. Life on board a naval ship is all about "class." Even the ranks signify this: 3rd class, 2nd class, 1st class, officers etc. Just as on the HMS *Titanic* there is a difference between third-class and first-class living arrangements, and, like Jack, I was surely out of my element as I ascended up the many levels of the ship. I continued until I finally came to the radio shack. Yes, that's where the name "radio shack" came from for the now-closed retail electronic store.

Upon entering the radio shack, Radioman First Class Bucker (RM1 Bucker) looked up at me and asked "Spector?" As he handed me the phone, he said, "It's Senior Chief Daniels, your detailer." I nodded as I took the phone from his hand. "This is Petty Officer Spector," I said with a smile, because I had a pretty good idea what was coming. A navy detailer is the person who cuts your orders. They are charged with filling the job vacancies (called billets) throughout the navy. Most sailors never get the chance to talk to their detailer throughout their entire career, either because they don't know one exists, or they don't believe they are allowed to speak with them. Not until you reach the higher ranks in the navy do you become aware of the importance of having a good relationship with your detailer. I was learning this lesson very early on.

To cut to the chase, Senior Chief Daniels was calling to make sure I was ready and willing to be cut orders to Recruit Training Command, Great Lakes, Illinois, as a company commander (now called a recruit division commander or RDC). I was going to "push boots" or, more formally, train recruits. Other branches of the military call it being a drill instructor, or DI for short. It was my dream job in the navy!

Unfortunately, landing that position was against all odds. Let me explain.

About two months prior to this phone call, my brother had called me from Great Lakes where he had just begun *his* tour of "pushing boots." He told me how he loved the job, and how it would be cool if we were "pushing boots" together. Of course, I loved the idea, but also mentioned that so many things were against me. While you could technically be an E-5 (2nd Class Petty Officer) and push boots, the navy preferred E-6 and above. No E-5s was the unspoken rule. As a deterrent, if you were an E-5, you had to be evaluated among the top 10% of the fleet. You also had to get the blessing of your current division chief (because they would be losing an able body), as well a recommendation from the ship's captain. The ship's captain? Hell, on a ship of over 5500 personnel, I never even met the captain, so why would he give me a recommendation? But the obstacles didn't stop there. Because of my rate (job classification), I was required to spend at least six years on ships before I was allowed to spend two years on a shore installation. It was called sea/shore rotation (SSR). As a machinist mate, my SSR was six and two, and I was only currently at three years of sea duty. I still had another three years of sea duty left before I was eligible for shore duty. Lastly, when I was initially assigned to the USS *Forrestal*, it was for a four-year billet (term). So, again, I had only fulfilled three of those four years. The odds were stacked against me. After explaining all this to my brother, his response, while lacking the energy he initially had at the beginning of the call, was, "Well, you never know until you try. I'll call my detailer for you and see if there is anything he can do."

I wanted this job more than anything, so that evening I went out and purchased a cassette tape (if you remember what those were) that would help me meditate. I don't remember the name of the audio tape, but I vividly remember the visualizations it instructed me to create in my mind while I meditated on the dream job I wanted. I pictured myself wearing the uniform, and saw in my mind all the details of that uniform. I imagined doing the job of a drill instructor and interacting with those around me. The entire guided meditation lasted about thirty minutes, and I went through this process day after day, sometimes twice a day. Anytime I had a free moment to spare, I closed my eyes and played this tape.

Well, I'm sure you figured out by now that I got the job. They gave me a waiver for the three years I still had on my sea/shore rotation, as well as the one-year waiver for my current billet. The captain of the USS *Forrestal*, called me up to his cabin, spoke with me for about fifteen minutes, and wrote me a wonderful recommendation. Lastly, my division chief told me not to expect my new orders for a few months, since I still had to fulfill my current four-year tour on board the USS *Forrestal*. Well, I got the orders in six days, instructing me to report for duty in three weeks at Recruit Training Command, Great Lakes!

Call it what you want—divine intervention, the Law of Attraction, a universal power—it doesn't matter. But I will tell you, whatever *it* is, *it* works. Perhaps meditation just puts you in the right frame of mind to take action in a certain way. Perhaps seeing and believing in your mind that you have already accomplished your desire somehow brings about its manifestation. Whatever your reasoning might be, meditation and visualization keeps you focused on the task at hand. Having a laser focus on your desires and what you want to achieve works! There are many types of meditation, on a wide variety of topics. I prefer the "guided meditation" as it keeps me centered and focused on a specific outcome. I have listed some of my recommendations in the resources section of this book. So, seek out different ways to meditate that work for you and *use them daily*. Even if you meditate only for ten minutes before bed each night, the compounded effect over time will have a drastic impact on your life.

1. **Become an avid reader:** Another method of personal development is to become an avid reader. While we are on the subject, let me thank you for picking up this book and beginning your journey towards becoming a life-long student of personal development. I know people are busy, and I hear the "I just don't have enough time to read" excuse a lot! But anyone can find the time to read. Here are a couple ideas you can implement, starting today, to help you become an avid reader:

   a. *Choose something you enjoy*: I have a list of recommended books in the resources section of this book, as well as a few I have mentioned throughout these pages. But you have to read something that you *enjoy*. I hate it when companies have "required reading" for their employees (unless, of course, it's one of my books on that list), because programs like that can turn people off from reading altogether. If you start reading a book and it's just not clicking with you, put it down and find another. Toss the book away, but don't toss away the habit of reading. Lastly, make sure the book is an *investment in yourself*! I'm not saying to stop reading the romance novels you love so much, or to stay away from the next Steven King release. If you are reading those books you are already an avid reader. But make sure it's a book that will improve *you* as a person and a leader, one that will help you become a better parent or mentor. Because not only is it an investment in yourself, but, when you implement the things you learn, you start to feel better about yourself; and when you feel better and become more confident in your abilities, you will keep on reading!

b. *Read ten pages a day*: As I have mentioned, if it's difficult to find the time then set a goal to just read ten pages of a good book each day. That's it, just ten pages. The average person can read ten pages in ten or fifteen minutes! When you multiply that by 365 days, that's 3650 pages a year, which equates to a lot of books in a twelve-month period. Again, remember *The Slight Edge* and how the compounding effect can really make a difference? This is a perfect example. Additionally, you can keep a different book in different places. In other words, keep one in the car (if you work on the road) to read during lunch, and/or keep one at the office for the same purpose. Most people will take a lunch break, but they never think to get in those ten pages at that time. It's the perfect opportunity to work on *you* while you're working on your job. Heck, pop-in your headphones and listen to your book on Audible while you go for a brisk walk. Which brings me to my next idea …

c. *Drive-time university*: Did you know the average person drives about twenty-five miles and spends about an hour behind the wheel of their car each day? This doesn't include the Saturday trip to the beach or the evening family dinner, let alone the weekend road trip to visit relatives. As Americans we spend nearly 6% to sometimes up to 10% of our lives in our cars, so why not make the best of it? It's called drive-time university.

What were once known as "books on tape," designed for those of us who were falsely considered lazy or *didn't like to read*, have now been transformed into the accepted format called the "audio book." The advent of the internet and digital age, which has forever changed the music and movie industry, has now begun to transform the publishing industry as well. It wasn't long ago when your only two options when purchasing a book was the hard cover or paperback. Fast forward to today. While those two options still exist (for now), your choices have been extended to include the *ebook* and *audio book* formats. In short, audio books are the new norm. They are hip! They are my preferred way of investing in myself when it comes to reading. Yeah, I know I'm not actually "reading" the book myself—   someone is reading it to me—but I love the fact that most times the author himself or herself is actually doing the reading! How cool is that? It's like they're right there with you! Why would you want to listen to the negative news or a radio station that repeats the same hit songs every twenty minutes or so when you could be learning something new? Why inundate yourself with pointless commercials and jingles when you could be spending that time improving your skills or abilities? I recommend downloading an application called Audible, or any of the popular audio book players, to the mobile device of your choice. Most cars today have *Apple CarPlay* or *Android Auto,* both of which interface beautifully with your mobile device. Every time you have to take a little drive, listen to an audio book. What I love about these apps is there is no need to hit the stop, pause, or save button when you arrive at your destination. These audio books automatically bookmark where you left off so every time you get back in your car, it will automatically start up where you left off, much the way your GPS will continue your route guidance. My wife and I both use Audible in our vehicles and we constantly take turns reading (okay, listening) to each other's books. It's become so much a part of our lives, our kids have now become accustomed to it as well. So, get the app, download your favorite book and turn your vehicle into drive-time university! You'll be glad you did!

2. **Study Your Inspirations**: *If you want to become part of the top 5%, why follow the other 95?*

    The word *success* can mean many things to many people. We all have our own definition of what it is to be successful, but regardless of how you define your success, one rule stands true: *if you want to be successful, do what successful people do!* No one becomes successful without being inspired, so you need to seek out those you admire, those few individuals who inspire *you* and study their teachings. This fits with *changing/improving your associations* which we discussed in an earlier chapter, only this time we are talking at an intellectual level. For example, let's say you are reading a book called *The Five Temptations of a CEO* by Patrick Lencioni, and it really hits home with you. A lightbulb goes off in your head that really inspires you. You enjoy the book so much, you can't help but tell others about it. Well, go out and find other works by the same author! Chances are you will enjoy them just as much. By the way, Patrick Lencioni is on the top of my list of recommended reading when it comes to leadership and navigating the corporate environment. He's written many best sellers, but *The Five Temptations of a CEO* is one of my all-time favorites. I highly recommend you pick up a copy for your library. I have mentioned many of my inspirations throughout this book, and you will find a complete list in the resources section, but the point here is: you need to find the ones that click with you and study their works.

A lot of books on the market today will advertise the "secret to this" and the "secret to that" but, unfortunately, most don't come through on their promise. So let me tell you a real secret to success. There are just as many definitions of success as there are paths to get there, so everyone's journey is different. That is true. However, you will soon find out that the more greats you study, the more you focus on personal development, the more you focus on *you*, a pattern will begin to emerge. You will begin to see *similarities in the teachings across all the greats*, from Napoleon Hill to Tony Robbins, from Wallace D. Wattles to Rhonda Byrne, from Jim Rohn to Bob Proctor and Dr. Joe Vitale. These similarities are the keys to *your* success and happiness! You can't just be told once what they are and expect drastic change. Sometimes you need to hear that message numerous times in different ways before the lightbulb finally goes on because the similarities have to do with your thought processes. You have to discover the similarities for yourself, because the journey will differ slightly from person to person. What resonates with me may not resonate with you in the same way, or on the same level, and vice versa. And that's okay, because we are all wired differently.

So again, seek out the greats, study their teachings, *discover those similarities* (some of which are presented in this book) and implement them! I challenge you to research any extremely successful person today, and I guarantee you they are life-long students of personal development. It's simply a part of their daily life. Michael Jackson's song "Man in the Mirror" comes to mind. Let that sink in.

Points To Remember:

1. *Know the details of your ambitions!* You must understand what it's going to take to achieve a goal and focus on those specific tasks to get you there. For example, don't just say, "I'm going to be a better manager." Instead say, "I'm going to be a better manager by doing A, B and C." Lay it out. Write it down!
2. *Have a definite purpose.* When you are confident in your purpose and direction, you exert a positive *energy* that is contagious, magnetizing and energizing.
3. *Any goals you launch* that focus purely on acquiring material things do not have the fuel needed to complete the journey. "One doesn't become wealthy because their goal

was to become wealthy. One becomes wealthy because they bring a *wealth of value* to the marketplace." (Richard Spector)

4. *What is the major difference between a pipe dream and a goal?* One is in writing, the other is not.

5. *The top 5% knows* if you are *happy* and grateful *now* for the things you have and the life you have, other things you can be happy and grateful for will come to you.

6. Personal development: "Work hard at your job and you'll make a decent living. Work hard on yourself, and you'll make a fortune!" (Jim Rohn)

7. *Meditation is a conscious practice* of informing and instructing the subconscious mind to deliver a desired outcome or manifestation.

8. *Become an avid reader.* Read ten pages of a good book every day and you will see the compounded results increasing your skills and abilities, launching your career upward!

9. *Study your inspirations:* Take the time to study those who have already achieved what you want, but, more importantly, study those who inspire you.

10. *Study the greats!* As you do, you will begin to see *similar elements or messages* in the teachings across all the greats. It is these specific similarities that are the secrets to *your* success and happiness!

Chapter Eleven - Rise Above and Take Action.

" Argue for your limitations, and surely they are yours!"
(Richard Bach)

Perceived Limitations:

White, black, Hispanic, Asian, Jewish, Christian, Buddhist, Muslim, rich, poor, northern, southern, city slicker, hillbilly, college grad, high school dropout, conservative, socialist … the list goes on and on and on. If you feel this list is downright exhausting, then you have received my message clearly. The labels of today are endless and relentless. We live in a world where most times we are forced to be like the Steady Eddie and jump on the train with the most votes or popularity at a given time and place. We are sometimes expected to act a certain way because of the very labels we ourselves, or society, places upon us. Perhaps your parents and/or their parents have taught you that because of your color or religion, you are less fortunate than others. That because you're a woman, you will never make as much as a man, or because you are black you don't have the same opportunities as a white person, or because you don't have a college degree you will never be as successful as those who do. It's called living in victimhood. That way of thinking needs to stop *within you*, right now!

I'm not here to tell you how to stop racism or bigotry or how to fix any other unfair practices that *some* people in this world may take part in. I'm here to tell you that the *labels* imposed on you are irrelevant! I'm here to help you get around those perceived limitations, because that's exactly what they are … *perceived limitations!* Now before you get all upset by that statement, let me explain. I didn't say any of these limitations weren't real. There are people out there that do treat certain people differently based on all kinds of reasons, but it's not everybody! In fact, the majority of people around us are good people. But if you believe with all your heart that you will never be as successful as the next guy, because of a specific label, upbringing or whatever, then guess what? To quote the fictional Aladdin's genie, "Your wish is my command." In other words, if you are of the mindset that you are a victim of society, then that's exactly what you will be for the rest of your life. You must rise above victimhood, and, to do that, you must take responsibility for everything that happens to you. We will discuss that in more detail in just a moment.

Imposed Limitations:

Do you think Barack Obama believed he would never become president because he was black, or Mary Barra believed she wouldn't become the CEO of General Motors because she was a woman? Let's not even begin to talk about Oprah. Now you may be saying to yourself, "Well, those people are the exception not the rule." Once again, if that is your train of thought, then you own those limitations! I'm not just talking about famous people here. There are millions and millions of very successful executives and entrepreneurs who are living the lifestyle they want regardless of any labels and/or obstacles society may have placed in their path. The only difference is what you do when faced with one of those obstacles. If you think those perceived limitations discussed earlier are tough, let's take a look at some imposed limitations that are, or should I say *were*, written into law.

I remember a time when women were not allowed to serve on board combat ships in the navy, yet today they do, and we even have female fighter pilots! I remember a policy where you would be discharged from the military if you were gay. That changed to a "don't ask, don't tell" policy. Now gays openly serve proudly in the military. And the granddaddy of all: just a little over fifty years ago, black people could not vote. Can you believe that was only fifty years ago? Today, they successfully hold political office in all branches of government, at all levels, including president of the United States.

In summary, to quote Jim Rohn once again, "If you really want something bad enough you'll find a way, if you don't you'll find an excuse." You need to reject the labels and the limitations attached to them if you truly want to be successful. Don't accept the fact that you will never be a model because you're a size six. Don't accept the fact that you will never be a famous radio DJ because you lack the midwestern dialect, or you have a southern drawl. Don't accept the fact you will never be a vice president or president of a company because you're a high school dropout, or you don't have a college degree. This is what Richard Bach meant when he said, "Argue for your limitations, and surely they are yours." If you believe you can't be the president of a company because you don't have a college degree, then you can't be the president of a company. *You choose to argue for, or against, your perceived limitations.* So always—always—argue against them.

The Blame Game:

So how does someone overcome these limitations and pull themselves out of that victimhood mentality? How does someone go about making these perceived barriers irrelevant, or, at the very least, easy to conquer?

Most people within the 95% like to blame everything and everyone else when things don't go their way. They get caught up in what I call *The Blame Game* where nothing is their fault. "My boss was an asshole," "The Landlord wasn't fair," "It's because he lied to me," "They didn't give me enough time to complete the project," "The company doesn't care about their employees," "I know I'm always late, but traffic is horrible." Coming up with excuses about why we failed at something, or why we aren't achieving the things we want, becomes a dangerous habit. Psychologists say that, at a subconscious level, we try to protect ourselves from anxiety and shame. So, for example, when the question "why were you fired?" is asked, you will hear responses like: "My boss didn't like me" or "They didn't train me like they promised" etc. Rarely will you hear: "I was always late" or "I did a horrible job and didn't pull my weight." The problem is, the more we keep giving these unsubstantiated reasons or excuses (playing the blame game), the more we are impeding our ability to succeed. When the blame is continuously shifted away from ourselves and towards someone or something else, we are programming our brain to believe:

"I'm not in control, and there's nothing I can do next time to change the outcome." We go through life living in this victimhood mentality because, in a way, it makes us feel better about ourselves or our current situation. Unfortunately, while it may ease some anxiety and make us feel better temporarily, it does nothing to pull us out of that rut and propel us forward.

How do we rise above victimhood and put ourselves in complete control? There is only one way: *You must take 100% responsibility for everything that happens to you.* And I mean *everything!* The relationship with your spouse or partner, the $10,000 in credit card debt, having to live paycheck to paycheck, even being in a job you hate. You must accept that it's all your fault. You must accept 100% responsibility for your current situation and own it, if you are to gain control of it and make changes. To put it another way, your current situation, good or bad, is the result of your past thoughts and actions. As the Law of Attraction states, *like attracts like.* If you say to yourself, "Well, I didn't attract the asshole boss" or "I didn't attract all this debt," I'm sorry if this hurts a little bit, but I'm going to tell you straight up, you *did* attract it. *Whatever your current situation, you chose to be there.* I know this is a difficult pill to swallow, and I know having a bad boss may not have been entirely your fault, but once you accept this concept of *full responsibility*, your life will begin to transform.

So how does all this relate to *The Executive Arena*, and why did I even include such a sensitive chapter? Because those around you can easily pick up on your attitude if you are in a phase of victimhood. How you react to certain situations, what you say and do when confronted with one of these "limitations," is all being observed and mentally recorded by those around you. It all ties back to *Perceptional Messaging* and the need to control what others perceive. You may be saying, "But this isn't fair. People should not be judged by their color, gender, religion, sexual orientation, weight, geographical location, etc.," and you are right! I agree with you 100%. But, regardless of the progress America has made towards equality, we still have a ways to go. There will always be bad people. Not to the degree the media would lead you to believe, but they are out there, and I've witnessed this firsthand. But until that day comes when we all live in perfect harmony, *you have a choice*. Either argue for your limitations or reject them and rise above them. Either live in victimhood and succumb to society's labels, or break through that proverbial wall, achieve the success you seek, while clearing a path and becoming an example for others to follow.

Points to Remember:

1. "I will become a success not in spite of your labels, but because of your labels. For they are my fuel." (Richard Spector)
2. You must take 100% responsibility for everything that happens to you.

Epilogue

A s I bring this book and *Part One* of our journey to a close, I wanted to let you know that I have truly enjoyed our time together, and I hope you have as well. This first book in the *Arena Trilogy* was designed to share with you those skills and aptitudes that would usually take years for one to learn and experience. I hope I have greatly shortened the learning curve, giving you the tools needed to *gain the advantage* over other aspiring and even experienced executives. You should now recognize that being acutely aware of your surroundings, including the actions and perceptions of those you interact with on a daily basis, is critical to sustained success in today's corporate environment. You now have the *armor* to protect yourself from those who may set out to harm or hinder your career progression, as well as the ammunition needed to fight for your dreams and achieve the success you so rightfully deserve.

However, from *Social Astuteness*, to *Perceptional Messaging*, from *Changing your Associations* to *Selecting and Using a Confidant*, none of these tools will be beneficial if you don't put them into action. I've known many people that have spent hundreds if not thousands of dollars attending seminars, or spent hours reading books on how to do this or do that, never putting the very things they have learned into action. *Knowledge is useless unless you can transform that knowledge into wisdom* and the only way to do that is to apply what you have learned.

We have all heard the phrase *knowledge is power*. However, if that were true, the college professors of the world would be millionaires. Applying a certain skill in a *real-life situation,* thus observing and experiencing the *results* of that applied skill, is where wisdom is obtained. To put it another way and going full circle back to the game of chess: *knowledge* is knowing which piece to move next; *wisdom* is knowing which piece your opponent will move next, based on your actions. So, take action and apply the things you have learned throughout this journey, even if they are only small steps. The next time you go to work, dress a little better, walk a little taller, and listen a little more. Absorb the conversations and situations around you, and always, always keep your ultimate goal at the forefront of everything you do.

Finally, once you feel you have mastered the skills presented in this book and have become a formidable opponent in *The Executive Arena*, you will be ready for our next journey together, *The Leadership Arena.* Too often, those in management positions believe leadership is simply being the boss, telling others what to do. They use the words leadership and management interchangeably, as if they were the same thing. They are not! In this second installment of the *Arena Trilogy*, we will discuss what leadership truly means, and the vast differences between managing and leading. I will share with you in-depth experiences from the US Navy as an RDC, recruit division commander (drill instructor), as well as the corporate world, including such topics as Job Alignment,

Positive and Negative Motivational Techniques, Leading through Mentorship and much more! Until then, I wish you much success and I would love to hear from you. Please feel free to email me through my website at www.arenatrilogy.com and share with me any successes you have along your journey to the top. I will personally answer your emails, and I look forward to embarking on many more journeys together. I may even use your story of success in a future book. Please feel free to visit the resources page, both in this book and on my website. Wishing you much success in all your future endeavors. -Richard Spector

Resources

Study the greats! Below is a list of resources I highly recommend. From authors to trainers and motivational speakers, below are some of the greats I have personally studied.

- Jack Canfield: www.jackcanfield.com: best-selling author (*Chicken Soup for the Soul*), motivational speaker and corporate trainer. Simply the best!

- Rhonda Byrne: www.thesecret.tv: author of *The Secret* and many other books. A must read.

- Jim Rohn: www.jimrohn.com: one the best speakers and success stories of all time. My personal favorite when it comes to success in life and business.

- Jeff Olson: www.slightedge.org: author of *The Slight Edge*, motivational speaker, entrepreneur, who had a huge impact on my life. Jeff was one of my mentors.

- Dr. Joe Vitale: www.mrfire.com: from homeless to multi-millionaire, Dr. Joe Vitale is a best-selling author many times over.

- Patrick Lencioni: www.tablegroup.com: author of the best-selling book *The Five Temptations of a CEO* and many others. Patrick is a leadership guru!
- Napoleon Hill: author of all-time best-selling book *Think and Grow Rich*. A must read!

References

Canfield, J. (2018). "Vision board ideas & how to make yours better." Retrieved from http://jackcanfield.com/blog/how-to-create-an-empowering-vision-book/

Flaxington, B. D. (2015, December 29). "5 reasons why new year's resolutions fail ..." *Psychology Today*. Retrieved from https://www.psychologytoday.com/blog/understand-other-people/201512/5-reasons-why-new-year-s-resolutions-fail

Furnham, A. (2018, April 10). "Savvy and skillful: A new look at office politics." *European Business Review*. Retrieved from http://www.europeanbusinessreview.com/savvy-and-skillful-a-new-look-at-office-politics/

Gross, E. L. (2016, June 27). "8 managers share the best way to ask for a raise (and get it)." *Forbes*. Retrieved from https://www.forbes.com/sites/elanagross/2016/06/27/8-managers-share-the-best-way-to-ask-for-a-raise-and-get-it/

H, H. (). "The 31 benefits of gratitude you didn't know about: How gratitude can change your life." Retrieved from http://happierhuman.com/benefits-of-gratitude/

Harris, J. (2014). "6 reasons why golf is good for business." Retrieved from https://www.pga.com/play-golf-america/new-golfer/golf-good-business?cid=pgacomsocial_FBshare

Marcus, B. (2015, Jan 19). "The 9 most frustrating facts about office politics." *Forbes.* Retrieved from https://www.forbes.com/sites/bonniemarcus/2015/01/19/the-9-most-frustrating-facts-about-office-politics/#6b18250d1d2a

McGrath, J. (2008). "How office politics work." Retrieved from https://money.howstuffworks.com/office-politics.htm

Olson, J. http://Slightedge.org/. Retrieved from http://slightedge.org/

Rodgers, D. "How to tell if your company is hoping you'll quit." Retrieved from https://www.monster.com/career-advice/article/company-hoping-you-quit-0117

Ryan, L. (2016, September 13). "Never burn bridges -- except in these five cases." *Forbes.* Retrieved from https://www.forbes.com/sites/lizryan/2016/09/13/never-burn-bridges-except-in-these-five-cases/